Carolyn Moore, in *When Women Lea* giving us a remarkable and practical road map for effective ministerial leadership as a woman empowered and blessed by God. This book is stunningly honest about the obstacles but equally hopeful about the possibilities when the church empowers all for ministry. I encourage pastors and laypersons alike to read this book, which is an honest story of one woman's journey and also points to a larger pathway which all women called by God for pastoral leadership can joyfully follow.

TIMOTHY C. TENNENT, PhD, president,
Asbury Theological Seminary

This is the book the church has needed—a book about women leading in the church that has no agenda other than a kingdom-advancing agenda. Carolyn's excellent work confronts our short-sighted, misguided, and confining moves that have kept half of Christ's ambassadors on the sidelines for too long. However, Carolyn's most significant contribution is in leading us in ways that we can take corrective steps so women can flourish as leaders and the kingdom of Christ can advance more fully. Many women will read this book. Every man should read this book.

BRIAN COLLIER, pastor, The Orchard Church

In a carefully written and engaging work, Carolyn Moore invites all Christians of whatever tradition to think through the timely issue of women in ministry in terms of both barriers and the strategies to overcome them. Developing a powerful theological argument by going back to the basics of Genesis 1-3, and thereby grounding the dignity and authority of women in ministry in nothing less than the glorious image of God, Moore is able to rightly connect the universal call to ministry from the Old Testament image of God to the New Testament proclamation of the universality of the gospel itself, especially as it is expressed in terms of Galatians 3:28. Moore's concluding counsel to a discouraged female minister toward the end of the book is poignant, gripping, and full of godly wisdom. I highly recommend this much-needed work.

KENNETH COLLINS, professor, Asbury Theological Seminary

Carolyn Moore captures the blessings and the struggles of being a woman in leadership, especially those who are strong in egalitarian and orthodox theology. She faithfully engages Scripture, her personal experience, cultural norms, and the latest sociological research. She carefully walks through the deficits women face in leadership roles and provides a roadmap for female leadership that is not defensive or tentative. This book challenged me and strengthened my ability to live out my calling to leadership within the church.

LEAH HIDDE-GREGORY, executive director of the Smith
Center for Evangelism, Mission & Church Growth

I want to get this book into the hands of all our women pastors—and all of our men, too! Equipped with research, we all can be better prepared for the unique obstacles that accompany women's opportunities. We will all have realistic expectations so hardships can be faced in a healthy way by everyone involved—the female pastor, her family, her congregation and its leaders, and her supervisors. I highly recommend *When Women Lead*!

LINDA ADAMS, bishop, Free Methodist Church

Carolyn Moore writes out of a deep well of experience describing the challenges and opportunities for women in Christian leadership. She begins by providing a biblical, theological understanding of women's leadership and then discusses many of the practical implications of the biblical case she makes. I enthusiastically recommend this book for women and men who want to know more about women's leadership in the life of the church.

DAVID WATSON, academic dean and vice president for
academic affairs, United Theological Seminary

Into a "manning up and womaning down" world, Carolyn Moore speaks a profoundly prophetic and pastoral word to the body of Christ about the calling and gifting of women for spiritual leadership. In *When Women Lead*, she champions a partnership between women and men for kingdom work.

JORGE ACEVEDO, pastor, Grace Church

WHEN WOMEN LEAD

Embrace Your Authority, Move
Beyond Barriers, and Find
Joy in Leading Others

Carolyn Moore

ZONDERVAN
REFLECTIVE

For Emmie Jo
When it's your turn, give 'em Jesus.

CONTENTS

Foreword by Tara Beth Leach ix
Foreword by Scot McKnight xii
Introduction: A Sign from God xv

Part 1: Barriers to Women Leading

1. The Theological Barrier..............................3
   What's the Bible Got to Do with It?
2. The Perception Barrier...............................21
   You See Me, I See You
3. Resources and Benchmarks 41
   Show Me the Numbers
4. The Pastoral Care Barrier 60
   She Loves Me, Yeah, Yeah, Yeah
5. The Biological Barrier...............................78
   The Very Real Thing Nobody Likes to Talk About

Part 2: Empowering Women
to Lead and Succeed

6. Identity 99
   Knowing Who You Are Is (Almost) Everything
7. Authority 117
   After You've Done All You Can Do, Stand
8. Equipping 136
   Real-World Stuff Everyone Needs to Learn
9. Partnership 156
   Why It's Okay for Men to Open Doors
10. It's All about the Kingdom of God 178

Acknowledgments... 193
Appendix: For Further Reading...................... 195
Notes 197

FOREWORD BY
TARA BETH LEACH

Years ago, I was diagnosed with iron deficient anemia, and I learned the hard way that a lack of iron can be tough on the body. I was always tired, no matter how much coffee I consumed. I was out of breath when I went up a single flight of stairs, and my hair was falling out. Anemia impacted my entire body, and I was functioning with little capacity.

Dealing with this condition has at times left me with "an anemic imagination"—a weak sense of what is possible for me physically, emotionally, vocationally.

What I have dealt with physically, I believe the church has dealt with theologically, when it comes to the role of Christians in God's mission throughout our world. Of course, both men and women are called to partner with God in the work of redeeming his good and beautiful creation! While the mission is God's, the invitation is for humanity to join God in this work. The apostle Paul outlines exactly how this is to happen in several of his letters, including 1 Corinthians 12 when he calls *all Christians* to do this through the impelling and propelling of the Spirit. The list of varying gifts the apostle Paul describes are diverse, because the mission of God is at stake and needs all hands on deck.

And yet, our imagination for what this ought to look like is anemic. We've lost sight of what can be. In many corners of the world, the preachers and prophets and apostles and pastors are male, while too often women are excluded from leadership roles. Women are not, however, excluded by the Spirit and the gifting of the Spirit. Sitting in our pews, board room tables, cubicles, desks, homes, and dinner tables are an enormous number of women with *anointed* gifts of the Spirit. They simply don't know it because they've never seen it lived out in bodies that look like theirs.

We are anemic.

We have been given the incredible gift and invitation to join God in the work of redeeming creation, but we are doing it at less than half of our capacity. When women don't lead in board rooms or preach in pulpits or sit at the decision-making-table, we are not fully leaning into the vision found in Scripture—the old school, not progressive vision, I might add.

I can't help but wonder what our world would look like if more women were not just welcome to the table, but emboldened to lead at the table, preach at the table, pastor at the table, teach at the table. You see, for me it isn't merely about equality, but about the mission of God we are all invited to join.

I'm thankful for women like Carolyn Moore who have been courageously living into their gifts. When I first had the chance to meet Carolyn after admiring her from afar for years, I saw an anointed and emboldened woman who desperately wants to see the church be the church Jesus said it can be. As you will discover in the pages of this book, when women lead as God intended them, the kingdom of God advances—that is, with women and men unleashed in the sharing of the whole gospel so that we might see God's kingdom in our neighborhoods, communities, churches, countries, and world as it is in heaven.

I pray that this book is found in the hands of courageous leaders who want to join women and men in this good and holy work. I pray that this book plants seeds in the imaginations of the anemic and nourishes the church to stand together as Spirit-empowered women and men. I pray that this book encourages the women who have gifts to teach, preach, and lead, and I pray that they would be emboldened to take the next faithful step in their calling. And I pray for a new day, the kind of day where books like this are no longer needed, the kind of day where our daughters find books like this on the shelves collecting dust. I pray that one day we would be the church Jesus said we should be.

Tara Beth Leach
Pastor, Christ Church
Oak Brook, Illinois

FOREWORD BY
SCOT MCKNIGHT

Carolyn Moore's *When Women Lead* is exactly what we
need—written by a woman who has planted a church from
the ground up, who had babies and children and teens, who
has a husband, who has people routinely asking her how
to defend women pastoring and leading, who realizes that
resources for women leading in ministry are not as plentiful
for women as they are for men, and who realizes through it
all that being a woman leader today is different than leading
as a man—especially in the church. *When Women Lead* is
not a response to the complementarian movement, nor is it
a biblical defense of women standing behind a pulpit or sitting in the leader's chair of an elders meeting. It's a pastoral
theology of leadership that should be read by every seminary
student. And by those who work alongside them in ministry.
And, in fact, by anyone who cares that women have a place
at the table.

    When Women Lead is about what it's like to lead as a
woman in whatever context God has called you to lead. I
loved this book, especially Carolyn's wit and wide-ranging

reading. She starts by showing how much of the conversation about women in leadership is based on a fall-accepting worldview when what we most need is a new-creation-based worldview that knows the kingdom of God, the very message of Jesus, has already been launched. A kingdom-shaped worldview starts in a different place—with redemption, with the power of the Spirit unleashed, and with transformation occurring. Because it does not begin with our fallenness but with the unleashing of the kingdom, *When Women lead* forms a different vision.

Carolyn also—and this was a painful reminder both of what I have heard and a painful unmasking of what I had not heard—informs us of the differing expectations for men and women in leadership, whether ministerial or otherwise. The odds are stacked against women (in case you didn't know), and the system is rigged. And while there have been some improvements in recent decades, we are far from fulfilling the vision of kingdom redemption for the sexes. What does it mean for a woman to pastor or lead in ministry while pregnant and giving birth? What challenges does she have with self-image and calling during menopause? Check, check, check. Each topic is unmasked and examined.

As a seminary professor, I believe many of my students think of church ministry as preaching sermons, teaching the Bible in Bible studies, and leading meetings. But ministry—in fact, all spiritual leadership—is first and foremost about people. It is about working with people. No two are alike, and not all of them are even likable. Ministry is mentoring and coaching people when not all want to bend in the direction you are headed. It's about pastoral care and holding hands and visiting people in the hospital, attending to unpredictable needs and predictable problems. It's about drug addictions and single mothers and cancer and divorces and marriages and pandemics. *When Women Lead* is a wise pastoral theology about what it's like for women to lead in the variety of different ways women are called to lead today for God's kingdom purposes.

Leadership is not always easy. It's a grind. There are weekly routines that demand attention, require expertise and wisdom, and never seem to let up. It can grind up a person as well, to the point where one's identity in Christ is lost. Whether your leadership involves speaking a prophetic word, a pastoral word, a rebuking word, or a wise word, you will find this an indispensable resource. It provides a comprehensive understanding of the kingdom, of calling, and of the many and diverse tasks of ministry and leadership held by women. Far from theory, this is the nuts and bolts of actual ministry.

It's a gift. One that will give more than you may be able to take.

Scot McKnight
Professor of New Testament
Northern Seminary
Lisle, Illinois

INTRODUCTION

A Sign from God

I'm beginning to think it was a sign from God.

Maybe that's because it *was* in fact a sign. It was standing in front of The Holy House of Prayer of Jesus Christ, a little building with burglar bars on the windows situated deep in the heart of one of the most impoverished areas of Georgia. The lettered sign held a string of announcements about repenting and where you can find the church on the radio. The last line on the marque, placed like a proverb across the bottom, read, "God have [sic] never called a woman to preach. Never will."

That sign was the kind of thing that ought to have downright agitated me. As a woman in ministry, I'm acutely aware that a remarkable amount of prejudice still exists around the issue of female leadership in the church. I don't hear it in every conversation, of course, but I have had enough experiences to know it is very real, and over the years I've developed a sensitivity to it. Even when it simmers beneath the surface, I often feel the inequity; sometimes it leaves me feeling trapped or angry. I find myself obsessing over biases encountered or talking way too often with way too much defensiveness about what happens when women lead.

That's why that beat-up banner in front of The Holy House of Prayer not only caught my attention the day I saw it, but in some odd way validated my feelings. It exposed my reality in such stark relief. The fact is, people unfairly, maybe even unknowingly, discriminate against women who lead. It is not just my imagination. What people like me experience is real, and that sign exposed the problem royally.

Sadly, it also exposed my own angry heart. That church, with burglar bars on the building, stood in the poorest part of town, in one of the poorest districts in Georgia. Rampant crime. Deep poverty, serious drug issues. But because bitterness had taken root in my spirit from years of experiencing inequity, I'd been too eager to prove a point that day. I took a picture of the sign and neglected to say so much as a prayer over the community.

Shame on me.[1]

How Do We Keep the Main
Thing the Main Thing?

Let that story and its moral lesson sink in deep. It captures the big message of this book. Women who lead often find themselves challenged by the inequities they face. They can become distracted by disappointments and find themselves with a defensive edge. Navigating a world of messages that subtly and not-so-subtly undermine their opportunities for leadership, they may also wrestle with their own internal messages of inadequacy. These interior and exterior perceptions of female leadership are just one of a web of challenges women face. Over more than two decades of dealing with many of those challenges firsthand, I find myself with a burning question worth exploring:

What barriers do women leaders face, and what strategies will equip them to lead past those barriers so they can lead effectively?

I know there are differences in how we lead and that those differences can be deeply discouraging to women. But my goal is not to do the literary equivalent of pointing to that street sign chapter after chapter so I can say, "Aha! It's true!" We don't need a sign or a book to make that point one more time. The world has met its quota of issues-based Christianity and victim-based posturing.

Here's what I believe we *do* need. We need a workable strategy for navigating beyond the theological mines and injustices of a fallen world, so we can spend our energy on what I failed to see beyond that sign: an impoverished community in desperate need of a fair account of the gospel.

If you're looking for a book that slams men (or the world in general) for not getting on board with the place of women in leadership, or that berates the church for acquiescing to yet another injustice by way of shoddy theology, you'll need to keep looking. What I hope you'll find in this book is a *kingdom* strategy for leading beyond the barriers—and by that, I mean a biblically sound, strategic plan that points toward and advances the kingdom of God. In other words, we're after a strategy that is wise but not political, thoughtful but not manipulative, strong but not angry. As we explore what happens when women lead—especially but not exclusively in the church—we aspire to be what Jesus might have called "wise as serpents, gentle as doves" (Matt. 10:16). In other words, we are looking for strategies that will intelligently and lovingly equip the church to respond to women's leadership and the pressures against it so we can strategically use all the resources at our disposal for the sake of welcoming and advancing God's kingdom on earth.

This is the point: to welcome and advance God's kingdom on earth. Underline that sentence so you don't forget what we're after. We aren't here to beat any drum or wave any flag other than Jesus. We want every leader called by God to be equipped and sent out for the sake of seeing God's kingdom come.

On the way to that goal, let's give a nod to two basic facts:

- **Fact #1:** We live in a fallen world.
- **Fact #2:** That world is full of people whose worldviews are more influenced by the fall (Gen. 3) than by creation (Gen. 1 and 2).

Those two facts end up being important to any discussion about women in spiritual leadership, because if fact #1 is true, then fallen attitudes will persist until Christ returns. If fact #2 is true, then building a theological foundation for female spiritual leadership based on creation principles becomes critical. *When Women Lead* is about what can happen when we take time to understand the fallen world while refusing to be governed by its limits. Everything I say in this book is predicated on a theology that is rooted in the "creation side" of Genesis 3. This means that we understand men and women to be partners in the work of creation, based on what we read in the first two chapters of Genesis (I'll say more about this in the pages ahead). From the first words to the last page of *When Women Lead*, I hope to challenge you to consider that men and women were created for partnership, and that our common goal is to become the answer to Jesus's own prayer—"Your kingdom come, your will be done, on earth as it is in heaven" (Matt. 6:10). When we unleash the whole people of God to share the whole gospel of God, the result is the welcome and advance of the kingdom of God.

That, ultimately, is what we're after. We're after the kingdom of God.

My Story

Let me back up a bit and tell you a little more of my story. I graduated from seminary and moved with my family to Athens, Georgia, in the late 1990s to serve as an associate pastor in a large downtown church. A historic vaudeville theatre stood just across the street from that church, and it seemed like a great place for contemporary worship, so I was charged with starting that service on behalf of the church. Who doesn't want to lead worship in a cool venue like that? I was smitten by the challenge.

The theater was beautiful. The people were treasures. The experience was miserable. I felt a little like the people who tried to put Humpty Dumpty back together. All the slick marketing and all the creative worship planning and all the sweat-producing sermon prep couldn't build a congregation. I had all the "want to" a person could bring to the task but found it impossible to reach critical mass in a 500-seat theater. I was completely unprepared for that kind of challenge. The worst of it was that I didn't have the good sense to quit. I'm not wired to give up on a challenge. Also, I'd never been part of planting anything new before, so I had nothing against which to measure my progress. Bless the dear people who hung in with me through nearly five years of that painful experiment.

Even though that first dip into starting something new was a mostly miserable experience, I caught the bug from it. When I was offered a chance to start a church from scratch, I couldn't say yes fast enough. I'd been itching to start another new thing for a while, but the regional church development officer of my denomination told me straight up that it had not been proven that women could plant churches. My hopes might have died there, if not for another denominational leader who found out about my interest. She asked if I'd be willing to plant a new church in Evans, Georgia. I realized this was probably my one shot at a new venture and, in the words of Lin-Manuel Miranda's Alexander Hamilton, (you've gotta see the Broadway show), I was not going to throw away my shot.

I moved to Evans with my husband and daughter in 2003. We were what you'd call in church-planting circles a "parachute drop," which means we'd been dropped into a community with no team or resources beyond a starting budget and timeline. We had to be fully self-supporting within eighteen months. No one believes the parachute model is a sane idea anymore, but back then, it was how many new churches got started. So we began. The church, called Mosaic, met for a few months in our living room, then moved to an office complex before settling in a school auditorium. Eventually, we moved into the front half of a warehouse that we shared with a retired businessman who used the other half to store his antique cars.

This is the part where I tell you all the good things we've accomplished, because I am a pastor, and pastors have a spiritual gift for bragging on their churches. What we have built under the power of the Holy Spirit is a very sweet missional community that serves our little corner of the world well. Because it is who I'm wired to attract, many of the folks who attend Mosaic have fallen through the cracks of more traditional congregations. In fact, many are first-generation followers of Jesus. Some have come to us from prison, jail, or addiction. Half the women in our church (literally half) are single, many of them with multiple dependent children in their care. We are also home to young families struggling to make ends meet and single adults with addiction issues. We have a former felon on staff, and the current chair of our vision team is a recovering addict (and both are doing fabulous jobs as leaders). We have worked hard to develop healthy leaders from among those God has sent into our community, and I am proud of the integrity and humility with which our leaders lead.

Now, I'll be honest with you. I know that last paragraph sounds like we are being the church just like Jesus said the church ought to be. To mission-minded ears, our demographics make us sound glamorous, but I need to be transparent here. These weren't the people I set out to attract. I am as competitive as the next person, and I wanted my church to look like all the other seeker-friendly church plants my colleagues were planting in that season when it was the "thing" to do. What I mean to say is, I wanted my church to be *big*. I figured if I could do the things they did— and I *could*—then I'd get the results they got. Never mind my gender. In fact, I was doggedly determined not to let my gender interfere with our ministry. I would serve Jesus and let him take care of our reputation. And Jesus, for his part, would give us big crowds with lots of people getting saved every week. That was the plan.

Or, at least, that was *my* plan.

I didn't understand how an inspiring vision plainly articulated would not yield the same results for me as it did for my male colleagues who were also starting churches. I did not take into account how hard it would be for a female pastor to attract leader-quality adults into our ministry. For that matter, I didn't realize how hard it would be to attract people *period*. (As my friend, Ben Witherington, said to me long after the fact, "What part of planting a church in the buckle of the Bible Belt didn't you understand?") Nearly twenty years in, our weekly attendance still runs around 200, far less than what I set out to build. As I'll unpack in later chapters, this is a pretty strong attendance figure for a female church planter, but that doesn't make it any less frustrating. For years, I was tormented by the question of why we could not seem to make this church what I'd envisioned. As do so many other overly optimistic spiritual entrepreneurs, I had every expectation that with hard work and a strong vision, I could be the female version of the next Insert-Current-Rock-Star-Pastor-Name-Here. It never once occurred to me to plant a *small* church—and failure was not an option.

In the absence of rapidly growing attendance, Mosaic grew deep in mission. We now worship in a warehouse that hosts both our church and a nonprofit we developed to house our local ministries. Our mission on the church side is to help broken people become whole, so we focus heavily on small-group discipleship, healing prayer, and recovery. Our nonprofit side is dedicated to building lives and breaking cycles. We host a thriving food pantry that serves veterans and low-and no-income adults with disabilities; a full-time, professional therapeutic ministry for children with special needs; and a volunteer-led weekly recovery ministry. GED tutoring and mentoring for low-income women help us to cultivate a culture of empowerment. All of this helps us guard against navel-gazing. Serving is in our DNA.

Mosaic is a small but effective fruit-bearing church, one I am honored to serve today. But church planting turned out to be much more difficult than I expected. What I didn't understand—*and what coaches and colleagues around me were not able to articulate*—was the role gender played in creating barriers to achieving my potential as a leader. Even when I could acknowledge it, I still somehow thought that if I worked hard enough, worked enough hours, and worked every day most weeks, eventually I'd make it. I was wrong. I worked sixty-plus hours a week for years on end and hit wall after wall. I signed up for every possible training opportunity. Nothing created the momentum I craved. I began to realize that a high-octane work ethic was no match for such barriers. Yet whenever I suggested that perhaps my challenges were at least partly connected to my gender (recognizing that male pastors have challenges, too), folks around me were quick to dismiss my hunches. "You're great!" they'd say. "It's not you! We love you!" As if that would make it all okay.

It's Not You (But It Sort of Is)

Over time, my frustration bred a kind of quiet insanity that kept me on an anxious edge (there is a statistic for this), but it also birthed a burning question:

What barriers do women leaders face, and what
strategies will equip them to lead past those
barriers so they can lead effectively?

This question propelled me into conversations around the country with denominational leaders, pastors, church planters, and women in sacred and secular leadership positions. I wanted to know if there were themes and patterns we had in common. While the weight of my initial study centered on female church planters, I discovered that my findings and their implications reach far beyond the niche ministry of church planters, or even of lead pastors. This journey has taught me a lot about what happens when women lead in *any* profession, and I want to share with you what I discovered. Along the way, I hope to inspire a few solid strategies to help both men and women unleash the potential that most assuredly exists among women who are gifted and called into leadership. I want to talk frankly about how the church can better support women leaders— not as a justice issue, but as a kingdom initiative. Equipped with the facts, women will be able to develop their own strategies to lead past the challenges and live into their created design.

Since I am a pastor, the stories I have to offer come mostly from that world, but I know women lead in many ways. I'm thinking about Jenni, the children's ministry leader who serves a missional faith community where there are far more kids being raised by single moms, foster parents, and grandparents than by married couples. She needs the scaffolding and support to raise up, organize, and resource volunteer teams for her atypical ministry. I'm thinking about Veronica, who leads a ministry in a low-and no-income apartment complex in an impoverished area. Newly appointed to this job, she needs to develop a holy rhythm that balances her enthusiasm for the work with her responsibilities at home as a grandmother raising her grandson. I'm thinking about Taylor, a young mother of two stepping into her first leadership role and feeling the stretch in her schedule, her emotional connections, and her physical health. I'm thinking about Heather, an administrative pastor working her way through seminary and leading a recovery group. Her great need is "voice"—a sense of *self*, the person God made, gifted, and called for this work of ministry.

This book is for all these women and for the student pastors, church planters, women's ministry leaders, small group leaders, and nonprofit directors who are up for the challenge of leadership and want to become all God has created them to be.

But this book is not only for women. As I've shared this information in seminary classrooms, with church leadership teams, in workshops, on stages, and in my writing, I've discovered that the men in the room are every bit as interested as the women in what it takes for women to lead successfully in ministry and beyond. For all the media focus on men who treat women immorally, I have found that the world is also full of faithful, ethical male pastors and leaders who want nothing more than to support and encourage women who have an authentic call to lead. This book is for them, too—men like Jorge, who pastors a large church with several satellite campuses led by women, and Doug, a coach trying to figure out how to make the most of women leaders coming into his network. There's Chris, serving as an associate under the leadership of a female pastor, and Mike, a layperson leading a team within a female-led ministry.

Our current culture makes it difficult for men like these to know how to best serve and partner with women who lead. The very public immorality of a few men—along with the current of complementarianism in America's evangelical culture—have left the faithful majority reluctant and uncertain about how to simply *be*.

This book is for all such faithful people, for the countless steadfast men and devoted women who are trying to live out the call to serve Christ well and who crave healthy partnerships in that work. It is for everyone passionate about seeing the kingdom come on earth, who are eager to see all our resources deployed for the sake of the glorious Revelation 7:9 vision: "After this I looked, and there before me was a great multitude that no one could count, from every nation, tribe, people and language, standing before the throne and before the Lamb. They were wearing white robes and were holding palm branches in their hands." This is the vision we're after—all of us healed, saved, delivered, and standing together before the throne of God.

What We Don't Know *Can* Hurt Us

All leaders face challenges, some personal and some systemic. Both men and women face gender-related challenges, and both are enriched by understanding more about what we all face as humans. As it turns out, what we do not know *can* hurt us. Unaware of the barriers that hinder growth and success, women and those in partnership with them will find themselves frustrated by the dynamics at work when women lead. Let's start with some sobering statistics.

Ed Stetzer and Warren Bird conducted what may be

the most extensive study to date on church planting in the United States. The study, completed in 2015 for LifeWay, estimated new-church failure rates at 32 percent after four years.[2] Their report offers a slightly higher rate of success than the rate for small businesses in general. What is most interesting is what happens to secular small businesses in years five through ten.[3] According to the Small Business Administration, 70 percent of small businesses that survive the first four years will still fail by year ten.[4] LifeWay's report may not have followed the trajectory out far enough to see the real rate of failure among new churches.

If there is a general risk to starting new ventures, that risk is increased for women. According to researcher Mere Sovick, women, "who own over 37% of all businesses in the United States, contribute significantly to the 50% small business failure rate,"[5] and that "small businesses owned by women cease operations 11% more often than businesses owned by men."[6] The Small Business Administration's statistical analysis of small businesses by gender affirms that women start businesses with less capital than men[7] and are under-represented in "high-patenting industries" (patenting is a measure of financial performance).[8] Sovick concluded his study by noting that women can decrease the rate of failure by acknowledging constraints to success, then exploring strategies to enhance leadership skills.

Read that sentence again so you don't miss the treasure in this pile of stats: *Women can decrease the rate of failure by acknowledging constraints to success, then exploring strategies to enhance leadership skills.* This is exactly what Stetzer and Bird discovered through their survey on church planting. They found that "the chance of survivability increases by over 400 percent when the church planter has 'realistic' expectations of the church-planting experience."[9] What is true for church planters is true for leaders in general—what we don't know *can* hurt us. Positively, to the extent that we know what we're getting into, we can hold more realistic expectations and employ more effective strategies. Women in leadership will universally benefit by understanding and openly processing the effects of the barriers highlighted in these studies. Women *should* lead and *can* lead, but they need better information about the unique circumstances they will face so they can adequately and strategically meet challenges head-on.

Let's Explore Some Ideas Together

The chapters in part 1 are grouped intentionally to help you think through what I call barriers (or challenges) women face when they take on leadership positions. In this section, you'll notice a lot of footnotes. Don't let that spook you. Instead, let it comfort you. What I want you to gather from the research is that the concepts we're talking about aren't one person's experience or even an educated guess. They're evidenced by reams of documentation, though little of it has trickled into the church.

Once we have explored the barriers women face when called into leadership, we'll move on in part 2 to develop a toolbox of best practices to build an effective ministry. What kinds of tools and training can be placed into the hands of women who are called to lead so that they have every resource at their disposal? We will unpack several areas of strategic equipping, beginning with identity and the critical importance of knowing who you are in Christ as the first step in taking authority in a world hostile to the calling of women. Then we'll talk about how to seek out men and women who can mentor, coach, and open doors to maximize women's opportunities for fruitfulness. We will give a little space as well for a discussion of Sabbath, play, balance, and personal renewal.

Let me also say something about the use of the word "gender" in this book. When I first began exploring the ideas we'll be discussing, the term "gender" was not nearly as loaded with multiple meanings as it is now. Today, "gender" often carries wider connotations, and while I want to acknowledge the different ways "gender" is now used in cultural conversations, I also want to honestly express my hesitancy to change my own language to appease linguistic trends. In every instance where I have used this term, please know that I am using it interchangeably with and defined as a person's biological sex. My theological and biological assumptions are such that while people deal with and define a range of gender-related feelings, there are only two sexes: male and female. We'll discuss gender in those terms—men and women, male and female.

But Seriously, Do We Really Need Another Book about Women Who Lead?

At this point, you may be thinking, *This is all well and good, but do we really need another book about what happens when women lead? Don't women already know the barriers they face?* I'm not sure they do. What if, as women, we really *don't* know what we don't know about ourselves? The surprise reaction and deep catharsis created by the #metoo phenomenon of 2017 (and the #churchtoo phenomenon that followed) is proof that much of what both men and women think about women, gender differences, and cultural norms is still remarkably under-processed. This may seem obvious, but as a dynamic of women's leadership, this is not something we've fully acknowledged and dealt with. "Most women are unaware of having personally been victims of gender discrimination and deny it even when it is objectively true and they see that women in general experience it."[10]

If women leaders are experiencing discrimination without an awareness of its presence, we have to assume they are internalizing its negative effects without even knowing it. Why would we want to leave anyone in that place? Meanwhile, when women openly confront the barriers to their leadership potential, "they feel empowered, not victimized, because they can take action to counter those effects. They can put themselves forward for leadership roles when they are qualified but have been overlooked. They can seek out sponsors and others to support and develop them in those roles."[11]

Every woman who leads—and every man intent on supporting her as a coach, mentor, supervisor, development officer, husband, lay leader, board chair, or partner in ministry—ought to have the benefit of hearing what it is like when women lead. Confident in who they are in Christ, they will be empowered to embrace the most effective leadership style and find permission to achieve the kind of rhythm that will sustain their calling over the long haul. They should have the opportunity to discuss with their team the barriers that have the most personal impact so that, with support, they can develop practical strategies for overcoming those hurdles. They should be encouraged to seek coaching or healing in areas of admitted weakness. When everyone is on the same page, the work can be accomplished with so much more grace and care.

We must continue this conversation because, as Maya Angelou famously penned, when we know better, we'll do better. Jesus himself said that truth is freeing (see John 8:32). Women who have been empowered with the facts will lead from a place of greater authority and treat others with more respect and less pressure as a result. How exciting to be able to help women reframe the circumstances of their leadership so that potential is exposed and anxiety is replaced by empowerment. Rather than "apologizing their way into the room," as one male leader quipped, women will learn to reframe challenges as opportunities so they can operate from a place of vocational strength.

It Is Time to Get (Biblically) Indignant

Do you remember the time Jesus touched a leper (Mark 1:40–45)? I love that story, especially how the leper challenges Jesus to help him:

> A man with leprosy came to him and begged him on his knees, "If you are willing, you can make me clean." Jesus was indignant. He reached out his hand and touched the man. "I am willing," he said. "Be clean!" Immediately the leprosy left him and he was cleansed.

Jesus was *indignant*, the NIV says, but there is some question about that interpretation. According to Bruce Metzger, of the 20,000 lines of the New Testament, only forty lines have questionable translations.[12] That means there is agreement among scholars about 99.6 percent of what we read in the Bible. Still, there are going to be a few hard words, some things we have to wrestle with. This word in Mark 1:41, translated in the NIV as "indignant," is one of those words. Whole books have been written on this one word. Curiously, almost every other version translates to "compassion," as in, "Jesus was moved with compassion." But we can't escape the "indignant" feeling inside the Greek word used by Mark.

Another scholar, Dr. Ben Witherington, tells me that the disputed word refers to the kind of feeling that comes from a person's gut.[13] He says the closest expression to the Greek is "the bowels of compassion." The feeling evoked is fierce and passionate. It is not just the *feeling* of compassion (like the sad face of a puppy on a get well card) but the kind of concern that *moves* a person to compassion.

There is *movement* in this brand of compassion. Jesus is not just aggravated at a disease or at a man brazen and desperate enough to challenge him to make a miracle happen. It seems to me that Jesus is moved by some feeling deep in his gut that remembers a fallen world and the unjust exclusion of lepers with no power over their disease. It slays me to think that maybe God inspired among the biblical writers the use of a word here that means both injustice and compassion, anger and identification—because a person can be fiercely moved by love to go after someone stuck in a pit and simultaneously be angry at all the things that got them there. Not all anger is without compassion, and not all compassion is without passion.

Maybe this isn't exactly a one-to-one comparison, but as a leader and a woman, I deeply feel the feelings in this story. I hear that hard-to-interpret word in the leper's story as our word, too. I know what it is like to feel a little like a leper before Jesus, challenging him to fix things so I can do what I've been called to do, and I am moved to help others who feel the same desperation. What drives me—and I hope what drives you—is this deep burden for women who know that they are called but who have lacked the right voices to encourage them forward. I feel their loneliness in their callings, and it moves me to do all I can to change the spiritual atmosphere in the church we so desperately want to serve.

I also feel a kind of biblical indignation toward our fallen world—I am fiercely moved to see it made right. I feel the deep weight of challenging a worldview held by literally half the Christian church.[14] I can feel God's compassion toward those who disagree with what I believe to be true even while I am indignant toward what got them there. I realize there are good and intelligent people who have wrestled with a few hard passages about the role of women in ministry in the New Testament and who have come to a different conclusion than I. Every time I share with groups of men and women about what happens when women lead, I am inundated with messages from spiritual leaders who tell me they are thinking through this freshly. While they agree with my findings at the heart level, they haven't taken time to lay their own biblical foundations for affirming women in leadership.

I tell them what I'm telling you: take time to do this work. The gospel depends on it, because the gospel is hamstrung by our lack of confidence in female leadership. We need to get a little indignant about that; we need to be moved at gut level to change the spiritual atmosphere for the sake of unreached masses who are desperate for Jesus to create a miracle in their lives. It is critical that we are grounded in our theology so that on the hard days, we are not missing signs of kingdom potential all around us. We must learn to see beyond our frustration to the vision of a realized kingdom where there is neither Jew nor Greek, male nor female, slave nor free (Gal. 3:28). May these pages empower and encourage you wherever you are in that journey. May they help you to stand and keep standing for the whole gospel of the coming kingdom. And may you take the authority given you, trusting that the kingdom of God is poised and ready to advance under your leadership.

PART 1

BARRIERS TO WOMEN LEADING

Do you remember our burning question?

What barriers do women leaders face, and what
strategies will equip them to lead past those
barriers so they can lead effectively?

Our study is designed with the two halves of this question in mind. We'll talk first about the barriers and then
about strategies to navigate beyond those barriers.

The first two barriers relate to how we perceive female
leadership, both theologically and culturally. I'll cover some
of what the Bible says about human design, men, women,
and leadership, but I'll leave the heavy lifting on that topic to
those who have covered this extensively in other places.[1] Our
focus is on understanding the tension caused for women by
those who hold an opposing view of female leadership and
how that tension affects a woman's ability to be effective

as a leader. How does it affect a woman's ability to gather an audience? Does it limit her opportunities to be properly resourced? How does it affect her posture at the leadership table? We'll talk about how female leadership is perceived both in and beyond the church and how that affects women's self-perception. We'll also touch on a fascinating phenomenon called *optimism bias* and how it affects the way we filter reality.

Then, we'll move on to more practical areas of leadership, addressing the lack of available resources due mostly (but not exclusively) to the fact that the market for women in vocational church leadership is very narrow. We'll talk about the unrealistic expectations placed on women leaders, who often find themselves working harder to reach the same goals as their male counterparts. And we will address more personal issues faced by women—for instance, their pastoral care style and what defines success for a woman (whether it is the culture defining success or the woman herself).

The last pair of barriers we'll discuss cover seasons unique to women from the childbearing years to midlife. These distinctive seasons in the lives of many women can present vocational challenges they will need to acknowledge if they are called to lead in an area of work that demands a large investment of personal time.

Enter into this study with a hopeful frame of mind. Yes, these are barriers we're discussing, but as we've noted already, a leader's chance of surviving hard times increases dramatically when she knows what she's up against. So what do we know and what can we learn about what happens when women lead?

CHAPTER 1

THE THEOLOGICAL
BARRIER

What's the Bible Got to Do with It?

"The plural of anecdote is not data."[1] So states a modern proverb, which sounds pithy and wise. Except that when you put enough anecdotes together, you not only have data, you've got a trend.

Consider this anecdote, for instance. I can't count the number of times in more than two decades of ministry that a newcomer to our church has come to me asking to talk about my place as a woman pastor. Of course, they don't ask me about this directly. Often, it happens after they've been visiting for a few weeks, and they'll stop me on the way out of Sunday worship or in the hallway as they pass by on the way to a group meeting. "Can I get an appointment with you?" they'll ask, casually, as if they've just thought of it.

But they haven't. They've been thinking about it nervously for a while. Based on what I know about them, I can almost always predict what's coming. They're wrestling inside, gathering evidence to settle what is unsettled. They want to like the church they've started attending, and they want to accept my place as their pastor. But something inside them can't make peace with this one piece of the puzzle. Or maybe, as they've raved about their new church to friends and family, something in the reactions of others has stirred up something inside them.

When we meet to talk, they'll spend the first few minutes telling me how much they love the church. They'll compliment my preaching, and they might even say something like, "You guys don't seem Methodist at all!" (Sadly, they mean that as a compliment; we get that a lot from people who don't expect to encounter lively worship and an evangelistic style in a Methodist setting.) Then, they get to their point. "I have no problem with women pastors," they'll say, "and I think you're awesome. But my mother/coworker/last pastor/ book I read/thing I've always believed since childhood has me thinking about it, and I guess I just need to know how it all works for you, you know—with what's in the Bible and all. Can you explain the part about women pastors to me?" Nine times out of ten, they don't actually *know* what's in the Bible. They haven't done any real research on their own. They just know what they've heard, and until now, they've had no reason to question it. But here we are, and now my job is to help them think through something they desperately want to be true, even if they can't shake the funny feeling that something is wrong.

I've had enough of these conversations to know there is an inner hesitancy to accept the place of women in leadership, especially spiritual leadership. In my conversations with women pastors and leaders around the country, I've collected dozens of stories just like mine. Women report noticeable pushback based on the theological opinions of those they seek to lead. It isn't always immediately voiced, but over time and upon reflection, almost every female pastor I've talked to has anecdotal evidence of brushing up against those who disagree theologically (sometimes ethically) with their place as spiritual leaders in the church. Sometimes it is as innocuous as the story I've just told. Sometimes it is accompanied by passive or not-so-passive aggression as folks vie for power in church leadership.

Maybe the plural of anecdote *is* data.

The point I'm making ought to be obvious. Literally half the Christians in the world—comprised of Roman Catholics, the Orthodox Church, Southern Baptists, and several Reformed movements—do not accept women in church leadership. Or, to spin it differently, almost all Christians have a strong memory of male church leadership while few have a strong memory of female church leadership. You'll hear me say this often as we discuss the barriers women face, but it bears repeating: the point isn't whether or not a barrier ought to exist. The point is that it simply *is*, and acknowledging it is the first step toward arming women to lead well. So what is the effect on women, beyond the obvious discomfort it may cause them, when so many people have a theological bias against them as leaders?

For starters, it means that women are fishing from half the pond. In the good work of building a church and seeing people come to Christ, women have the opportunity to influence far fewer people than their male colleagues because half the Christian church opposes female leadership. You may be thinking, "Yeah, but you're talking about

Christians when you quote these numbers. Isn't the point to go after non-Christians?" Absolutely. But a healthy church needs mature, healthy leadership, and a smaller pond affects the prevalence and quality of good leadership and the ability to attract top-level staff members. Because 50 percent of Christians do not take an egalitarian position (affirming women in ministry leadership roles), the available pool of laypersons and leaders to participate is much smaller. If you grew up in a Southern Baptist church or another denomination that prohibits women pastors, it will be hard to shake a bias against female leadership as an adult, even if you haven't been in church in years. To gather critical mass, women will have to cast a much larger net.

Still not convinced? Let's get beyond anecdotes to some cold, hard facts:[2]

- Nationally, 11.4 percent of churches are led by women.
- Just 5.1 percent of churches with a conservative theology are led by women.
- A National Congregations Study conducted in 2012 showed a slowing trend of women entering ministry.
- That study, which polls a representative sample of American congregations, reports that 41 percent of Americans believe women should not lead in a religious institution.
- This ideology skews higher in the American South, where 46 percent of all persons disapprove of women in religious leadership. Among conservative Christians, that number jumps to 58 percent. Interestingly, the study also took note of the size of congregations responding.

- The larger the congregation, the less likely the parishioners were to approve of women leaders. Only 32 percent of those attending small churches (with fifty or less in attendance) disagree that women can lead, while 78 percent of those in churches of more than one thousand in attendance disagree with female leadership.

Worldview impacts financial viability. Virtually every female church planter I talked to expressed deep concern about the financial health of her church. Yet when I polled women pastors about the financial health of their churches, they didn't immediately notice the correlation between their gender and the giving patterns of their people. When I asked, "Do you have any sense that your church's financial health is negatively influenced by your role as pastor?" 84 percent reported they were *not* negatively impacted. But that's a hard thought to swallow, given that many denominations do not believe women should be pastors. The math doesn't add up. Of course, the finances of female-pastored churches are affected. One woman was bluntly honest about the personal toll it was taking: "Do I deserve a raise? Hell, yes, I deserve a raise. But I know the church can't do it. And you know, a man might just make it happen, but I can't. I negotiate myself out of it, right?" The problem is that women themselves haven't been given enough space to reflect on their circumstances in such a way that they can receive and productively respond to their reality. Most are too busy just trying to survive.

This financial dynamic exposes what I would call a theological double bind. A 2013 MIT study revealed that while theologically conservative Christians give more to religious institutions, progressives give less to religious organizations and more to secular concerns.[3] In other words, while conservative churches led by women will receive fewer members because of their conservative theology, liberal churches led by women will receive fewer funds. So choose your worldview—conservative or liberal—and either way, women are on the losing end of the numbers. Meanwhile, there are people whom women pastors will never meet simply because of their gender, even if those same people have not fully explored the biblical underpinnings of an egalitarian position. Why? Because they'll never walk into a church led by a woman.

What You Believe Matters

Going back to my conversation with newcomers who are questioning what they believe about female leadership, I've noticed this: They don't want to hear the actual biblical arguments on female leadership as much as they want to hear that I *know* what's in the Bible. They want to know I've found my own peace and even confidence in my interpretation of Scripture. They trust my opinion, but they need to hear me articulate it. There are some who will remain skeptical even if they continue to tolerate my place as their pastor, but most just need a little reassurance. Most of the time, it isn't the explanation that convinces them but the Holy Spirit. This is not to say I don't believe in having good theology. On the contrary, I'm convinced that what you believe matters. Theology is important.

Most folks center the debate about women in church leadership around two New Testament passages written

by Paul to the early church—1 Corinthians 14:34–36 and
1 Timothy 2:12:

> Women should remain silent in the churches. They are
> not allowed to speak, but must be in submission, as the
> law says. If they want to inquire about something, they
> should ask their own husbands at home; for it is disgrace-
> ful for a woman to speak in the church. Or did the word
> of God originate with you? Or are you the only people it
> has reached? (1 Cor. 14:34–36)

> I do not permit a woman to teach or to assume authority
> over a man; she must be quiet. (1 Tim. 2:12)

Far better academics than I have written extensively on
these passages, so I won't spend time here exegeting them,
but there are common exegetical choices and decisions
interpreters make. These passages must be taken within the
context of the overall message of the Bible. They must be
read through the lens of Deborah's story (Judg. 4–5) and
through the lens of Mary's charge (John 20:18); through
the lens of Galatians 3:28 ("there is neither Jew nor Gentile,
neither slave nor free, nor is there male and female") and
the stories of Phoebe, Priscilla, Tryphena, Tryphosa, and
the great host of women who co-labored in the gospel with
Paul (Rom. 16). God has not called all women into vocational, pastoral leadership (nor has he called all men into
ministry leadership), but he has surely called us all to serve
the kingdom in the ways we are gifted. That women were
mentioned at all in the Bible is a testament to their dynamic
contribution to the early church and gospel story.

The problem is that we begin these conversations about

women in spiritual leadership in the wrong place. Rather than starting with Paul's epistles, we should begin in Genesis 1 and 2, in the opening pages of the story of God, because where we begin makes all the difference. The argument for female leadership within the church begins in the garden of Eden. The core theological question is this: Is the tendency to resist women leaders a fact of God's original, intended design or a fact of the fall? John Piper, a noted Baptist pastor and theologian, argues for God's design and intention for men and women and makes it clear that this created design is not just a matter for the home. "We are persuaded that the Bible teaches that only men should be pastors and elders . . . it is unbiblical, we believe, and therefore detrimental, for women to assume this role."[4] Complementarian arguments like this affirm a distinction between men and women and deny the full and equal partnership of men and women in leadership, asserting that from the beginning, women were designed to play the role of "helper" (Gen. 2:18), with the role of leadership reserved for men alone. An egalitarian view, on the other hand, argues that while the fall is responsible for setting man and woman against each other in an antagonistic relationship, God's intended purpose at creation was for man and woman to fight the battle of evil together as equal partners.[5] Indeed, the Hebrew term translated as "helper," *ezer kenegdo*—the same term used to describe God's relationship to his chosen people—lends itself to this interpretation.

Egalitarians and others who promote the full inclusion of women in church leadership read Paul's comments about women through the lens of the creation story—a narrative that didn't create hierarchies but gave us clues to the fulfillment of God's created purposes. Male and female experience this as partners in the work of realizing God's kingdom on earth, fulfilling each other's contributions to the kingdom:

> Then God said, "Let us make human beings in our image, to be like us. They will reign over the fish in the sea, the birds in the sky, the livestock, all the wild animals on the earth, and the small animals that scurry along the ground."
>
> So God created human beings in his
>   own image.
> In the image of God he created them;
> male and female he created them.
>   (Gen. 1:26–27 NLT)

The first creation story in Genesis describes the work of man and woman together. God blessed them and directed them to multiply and care for his creation (Gen. 1:28). This was their work *together*—to steward the rest of creation in partnership with one another. The clear hierarchy established in both creation stories of Genesis is the hierarchy of humans over animals, not male over female. Men and women are cut from the same cloth, as it were; their creation story is not a text of hierarchy or value but of unity and interrelatedness.

In his remarkable treatise on the theology of the body, Pope John Paul II explains that the word that spoke man and woman into existence is a word rooted in their *being*, rather than in their *doing*. What is good, John Paul II seems to imply, is that man "is," and not what he "does." The created goodness of men and women is not found in the roles they play but in their very existence, and it is the combination of the two sexes—male and female—that reflects the image of God.[6] Moreover, their relationship reflects an ontological equality as well as a functional equality.[7] To say this simply, men and women are *both* created in the image of God, and *both* are given the task of stewarding creation.

The fall, when humanity sins in Genesis 3, turns this partnership of equals into an antagonistic relationship. Adam and Eve, condemned by their failure to obey God, will now experience suffering in this life. Adam will fight against the ground, even as he works it for his existence. Eve will no longer have a partnership with Adam; he will rule over her. Neil Cole calls this "the failure of mankind, not the design of our Creator."[8] Genesis 3 describes what happens when the Enemy of God and humanity attempts and succeeds at distorting the created design. This narrative is *de*scriptive, not *pre*scriptive, and that makes all the difference. The great sadness is that our created purpose was weakened at the fall of humankind. We were meant to fight in partnership together against evil, but in his attempt to throw us off our game, the Enemy of God divided us so he could conquer us, and we've been trying to recover that unity and partnership between the sexes ever since.

What about the Rest of the World?

This broader narrative highlights the problem with rooting our debates in two or three verses written by Paul in the New Testament. If those "problem verses" were really the problem, then the bias against female leadership would be limited only to Christian circles, where people care what our Bible says. But the bias against women is a global and historic reality. Think for a minute about what women are allowed to do in other parts of the world. In Afghanistan, only 22.6 percent of women read.[9] Two-thirds of the world's illiterate adults are women.[10] The literacy rate for women in Pakistan, Nepal, India, and Bangladesh is less than 60 percent.[11] Compare that with our experience in the United States, where women outnumber men on college campuses. If you are a woman, the fact that you're holding a book in your hand right now puts you in a privileged minority. You should stop and utter a prayer of thanksgiving. Then pray for your sisters who don't read.

Now think about your relationships. In developing countries, an estimated one in three girls are married before the age of eighteen, and one in nine are married before the age of fifteen, with little or no say in the matter.[12] Four out of five victims of human trafficking are girls.[13] At least a thousand honor killings occur in India annually, with another thousand on average occurring in Pakistan.[14] Honor killings happen for all kinds of reasons. Maybe a woman refuses to marry a man she's been ordered to marry, or maybe she has dressed immodestly. Or maybe she has been raped, and for that crime committed against her, she can be killed.

Let's talk about rape and abortion. Women around the world aged 15–44 are more at risk from rape and domestic violence than from cancer, car accidents, war, and malaria.[15] American women are not immune, either. One in five women on American college campuses has experienced sexual assault.[16] One in three has experienced sexual violence in their lifetime.[17] And those are the women who make it to adulthood. China and India account for an estimated 1.4 million "missing female births" annually due to gender-biased sex selection.[18] In China, for instance, men outnumber women by as much as 34.9 million.[19] In India, an estimated thirteen women die every day as the result of an unsafe abortion, and most of them are aborting a female fetus.[20] That's one or two women lost to this world for every botched procedure. It is stunningly misleading to characterize abortion rights as a "women's health issue." It is anything but.

Women and girls fare worse than men economically,[21] and it isn't as if we're immune in this country. The US Census Bureau reports that in 2018, there were 38.1 million people living in poverty. Of those, 56 percent—or 21.4 million—were women.[22] This statistic goes deeper than the numbers. It is something in the way we are wired. A *New York Times* headline reads, "When Wives Earn More than Husbands, Neither Partner Likes to Admit It."[23] This finding also originated in the latest census report, where it was noted that when women make more than their husbands, they fudge their numbers and report less than their actual earnings while men fudge their numbers in the opposite direction so it doesn't look like their wives earn more. The people who evaluate census numbers call it "manning up and womaning down."[24]

Why do you suppose we do things like this? Is it because women really shouldn't make more money than men? Or are men's egos so fragile that they can't enjoy a woman who makes more money than they do? All over the world, human beings have a natural inclination toward "manning up and womaning down." What we learn from these statistics is that globally, how we view women is not a "conservative vs. progressive" issue. It is not an American Christianity issue, nor is it a specifically Christian issue. All over the world, we see the effects of sin disproportionately affecting women in ways that undermine their worth, value, and giftedness.

Let's make this personal. How do *you* personally view women and their place in the world? If you are a Christian, your answer should be rooted in how you understand the story of God and his relationship to his creation. That understanding will determine how the church will participate in the spread of the gospel and how women will be part of that story. It's all about the kingdom of God.

September 26, 2017. If you were a Saudi Arabian woman, you'd know this date by memory, as it was likely one of the most liberating days of your life. It was a culture-changing day for all Saudis: the day women in Saudi Arabia were given the right to drive (though the final directive would not fully materialize until mid-2018). This victory was life-altering for Saudi women, who are still discouraged from taking jobs that put them in contact with men.[25] Once, when Bill Gates was speaking to Saudi Arabian businessmen and political leaders, someone asked him how he'd suggest they improve their country's global ranking in the field of technology (it isn't strong). What, they asked, would Gates recommend moving them into the top ten nations globally for technology? Gates responded, "Well, if you're not fully utilizing half the talent in the country, you're not going to get too close to the top ten."[26]

He's right. Study after study shows that in every arena—economics, quality of life, technology, media, military, and, yes, religion—the advancement of a culture depends on how it values its women. Across the globe, humans systematically value males more than females, even in the womb. How do we begin dismantling this worldview? It's more than a couple of lines in the New Testament. Fundamentally, it's a matter of how we understand God, creation, and the world.

The bottom line is that the original design for men and

women is partnership, not hierarchy. Our embrace of gender hierarchy is a product of the fall. And if our embrace of a hierarchical worldview is the product of the fall, and not God's design, then the hard fact is that teaching alone will not "fix" it. This bias is a mark on the entire human race, a stain and a curse that has fallen on every cell of our world. Our grief over everything that is not as it should be is rooted in a deep longing to get back to the other side of Genesis 3. But try as we might, human effort alone cannot fix the fall.

Still, we try. We try with information. We want to educate everyone *around* a woman who leads, so they'll respond more positively to her leadership. This is how we've been conditioned to respond to injustice. But perhaps a more effective strategy is to start with the woman herself. Equip her with a solid creation-based theology, then give her the tools she needs so she can be confident in her call and take authority over the work for which she is anointed. Support her in forming partnerships where she can take on the worthy mission of transforming the world with Jesus. Only transformation can move this world back to the other side of Genesis 3, and only the Holy Spirit can do this transforming work. In this regard, Jesus's words are significant. His commands after the resurrection are gender-neutral: "Go and make disciples" (Matt. 28:19), "You will be my witnesses" (Acts 1:8), "Take up [your] cross and follow me" (Matt. 16:24). These commands and commissions were not given just to men. They were given to all his disciples—both men and women.

Just as Jesus said, "the poor you will always have with you" (Matt. 26:11), there will always be those who believe the work of women is best done in the home, within the bounds of family life, and certainly not in vocational leadership within a church. This is a difficult truth for women, perhaps all the more so for female spiritual entrepreneurs who aspire to new works. For women who lead, a strong egalitarian and orthodox theology, combined with a solid sense of Christ-rooted identity, is critical to withstanding the opposition and resisting the tides of uneducated opinionating.

The Damning Difference between Believing and Having an Opinion

Not everyone agrees with me, of course. As I've noted, half the Christian world rejects the egalitarian view of gender. A leading theologian and pastor in the Reformed and Baptist theological tradition cites the bias against women in leadership as proof that when women lead, they are working against their created design—that the very existence of conscious and subconscious resistance to women leaders is evidence that female leadership is not natural.[27] A study by Catalyst, an organization that promotes the integration of women into leadership, cautions that embracing this gender-biased line of thought can be damaging.

> Through the extensive research on gender differences and similarities, we learn that women and men are more similar than different and that there is more variation among women and among men than there is between women and men. By creating false perceptions that women and men are "planets apart," however, stereotyping results in women being overlooked for the top jobs—no matter how strong their actual credentials.[28]

Malcolm Gladwell's *Blink* is a brilliant book about how people think and make choices. In it, Gladwell suggests that people often struggle to arrive at consistently defensible conclusions when they are asked to replace their intuitive preferences with a carefully articulated decision-making process. To make his point, he describes an experiment by two researchers—Jonathan Schooler and Timothy Wilson—who wanted to measure how experts and non-experts judge an everyday product. Their study began with a *Consumer Reports* evaluation of strawberry jam.[29] A panel of food experts was charged with ranking forty-four different brands of jam using very specific criteria with which they'd be familiar. They were asked to comment not just on taste but on texture and other things an expert might notice but the average jam eater might not. Once the jams were ranked, Schooler and Wilson chose five jams from the ranked list—two highly ranked jams, one jam ranked average, and two ranked low. They then conducted a taste test among college students using those jams, only they didn't ask the students to use a ranking formula. They just wanted their unfiltered opinion of five jams to compare with that of the experts. The students' rankings were impressively strong. While their top two may have been in a different order than the experts', they still managed to know which of the five tasted best and which left more to be desired.

What happened next is why I'm telling you this story. Wilson and Schooler recruited another group of students to taste the jams, only this time they asked them to not only rank the jams but to say *why* they were making the choices they made. Why did they prefer one jam over another? What determined their choices? This time, the students bombed. The rate of agreement between the students and the experts was not quite 10 percent. As Gladwell noted, "By making people think about jam, Wilson and Schooler turned them into jam idiots."[30]

What is the lesson of this experiment? Surely it is not to stop deeper thinking or to suggest that thinking gets in the way of what we like. The lesson of this experiment, Gladwell says, is "about the loss of a much more fundamental ability, namely the ability to know our own mind."[31] The researchers learned that the unenlightened students simply didn't have the tools to explain how they felt about jam. When they tried, for instance, to explain texture (though they had no vocabulary or prior experience doing so), they ended up using terms that caused them to adjust their true preferences. Gladwell concludes,

> Jam experts don't have the same problem when it comes to explaining their feelings about jam. Expert food tasters are taught a very specific vocabulary, which allows them to describe precisely their reactions to specific foods . . .
>
> This does not mean that when we are outside our areas of passion and experience, our reactions are invariably wrong. It just means that they are shallow. They are hard to explain and easily disrupted. They aren't grounded in real understanding.[32]

What does this have to do with the theological barrier faced by women who lead? If you recall, I began this chapter by sharing a typical scenario wherein folks come to me, asking for my take on women in ministry, noting that a majority have not done their own research. Very few can quote the Bible on this topic; fewer still have read commentaries or done the exegetical work to form their own opinions. They just know what they've heard, and they find themselves questioning whether their participation in our church is in line with their hunches. The world is full of people I'll never talk to who are not convinced that women ought to be leading. What they are likely responding to (though they don't even know this is what is happening in the recesses of their mind) is their own fallenness—fallenness that makes us all prone to want hierarchies over partnerships. They have arrived at a position, but not by following a reasonable, researched path.

Felicity Dale, author, pastor and house church advocate, asks a poignant question: "There have been times when everyone knew God did not want women to lead in the church. Could there be a time when everyone knows the opposite is true?"[33] The first-century church proved that when men and women work together to build the kingdom of God, operating in freedom and in the power and giftedness of the Holy Spirit, the effects of the fall can be reversed, and the glories of the gospel will be exposed. I believe that can happen again.

CHAPTER 2

THE PERCEPTION
BARRIER

You See Me, I See You

Have you heard Heidi Roizen's story? Heidi is a successful venture capitalist in Silicon Valley who built her business using several relational practices that set her apart from others. In the world of technical innovation, networking and collaboration are not "business as usual" (remember this; we'll come back to it in chapter 10) and her attempts to collaborate with others earned her a good name in the tech industry.

Two Harvard Business School professors learned about Roizen's success and wrote a case study highlighting how she'd used networking and hospitality to build a positive reputation and a successful business.[1] Sometime later, two other professors, Francis Flynn of Columbia Business School and Cameron Anderson of New York University, took that case study and adapted it for use as an experiment in how we perceive gender.[2] What they did was brilliant. They simply changed the name "Heidi" in the narrative to "Howard" and changed all the pronouns from feminine to masculine. Everything else in the story remained exactly the same. Flynn distributed the "Howard" case study to half of a business school class and the "Heidi" case study to the other half of that same class. Students were instructed to read the case study and evaluate Roizen based on several standards. Flynn later said in an interview,

> As you might expect, the results show that students were much harsher on Heidi than on Howard across the board. Although they think she is just as competent and effective as Howard, they don't like her, they wouldn't hire her, and they wouldn't want to work with her. As gender researchers would predict, this seems to be driven by how much they disliked Heidi's aggressive personality. The more assertive they thought Heidi was, the more harshly they judged her.[3]

Meanwhile, people loved Howard. His assertiveness (the same level of assertiveness as Heidi, we should remind ourselves, since it was not just the same study but *the same person*) was seen as a positive. He was confident, clearly solid leadership material.

Are you surprised?

If so, you're probably not a woman. For many women, this is a familiar story. And Roizen's case demonstrates an issue at the heart of female leadership: the more successful a woman appears, the less well-liked she is.

Read that again.

It doesn't make sense, does it? And yet here we are,

still. As Solomon lamented in his pursuit of meaning, there is nothing new under the sun (Eccl. 1:9). Since the fall of humankind we've been measuring likability through the lens of distorted hierarchies. When women violate the norms of likability—say, by being more assertive than is usual for their gender—they pay a price in reputation. When they opt for being well-liked (in other words, more passive), they are seen as less competent. And that perception not only affects the ability of a woman to integrate into an organization, but also affects how she sees herself as a leader.[4]

But surely things have changed, right? Tell me this study is fifty years old. In fact, Gallup pollsters first asked Americans in 1953 whether they would prefer a male or female boss.[5] It should come as no surprise that respondents in that decade overwhelmingly preferred a male boss (66 percent), while only 5 percent stated a preference for a female boss. The rest of them said it didn't matter.[6] But in our generation? While we might have expected a radical shift in worldview, that hasn't happened. In 2014 when the question was asked again, the percentage of respondents who said they would prefer a female boss never exceeded 25 percent. Why is that, exactly?

The Double Bind: How Others See Us

We all have opinions about leadership and gender, whether we realize it or not. I've referenced Malcolm Gladwell's *Blink* already, and Gladwell shares some additional insights about both our conscious and unconscious attitudes toward gender. Gladwell says we tend to operate on two levels. We have our stated opinions—what we consciously believe and own—and then there is what we believe—perhaps even deeply, but not in a way we perceive.[7]

Take, for example, the story Gladwell tells of how women have integrated into orchestras. You'd think that in the arts world, talent and creativity would reign supreme in the selection of musicians. Surely no great artist would consciously believe that women are inferior to men when it comes to playing, say, the violin. Yet until relatively recently, orchestras were a mostly male-dominated world. It isn't that women never auditioned, but when they did, they rarely, if ever, won a seat. Was this because women are inherently less musically gifted than men? Or could it be that "female" wasn't the preferred option of those judging auditions?

This question sparked an experiment proposed by Herb Wekselblatt. Herb, who played tuba for the Metropolitan Opera in New York, suggested holding auditions where candidates played out of sight behind screens. His theory was that if auditions were blind, the judges would be free to hear the music without the influence of unconscious prejudice. The first time they tried it, all four winners of the auditions were women. As Wekselblatt noted, "That would simply never have happened before. Up until that point, we had maybe three women in the whole orchestra. I remember that after it was announced that the four women had won, one guy was absolutely furious at me. He said, 'You're going to be remembered as the SOB who brought women into this orchestra.'"[8]

That first experiment happened in the 1960s, and in the years since, screens have become commonplace at auditions. According to Gladwell, "The number of women in the top US orchestras has increased fivefold."[9] Why did blind auditions make such a difference? Gladwell's point is that we tend to make snap decisions from deeply rooted places of personal bias, even when we don't realize those feelings exist within us.[10] The shift to blind auditions for orchestras means that women now have access to a world previously denied them. They can be judged by talent alone. The experiment loudly makes the point that gender bias is not restricted by worldview. In other words, this is not a Christian issue or even an American issue (blind auditions are now practiced internationally, by the way, with the same positive result). The unconscious bias we have against women is a *human* issue—rooted in our human nature. Gladwell notes that "most of us have much stronger mental associations between maleness and career-oriented concepts than we do between femaleness and ideas related to careers."[11]

What does this mean for women who land positions in male-dominated fields (like a position of ministry leadership) or leadership positions wherein they oversee men? The business world has coined a term for what happens next. When a woman takes a position of leadership, she will find herself in one of two camps. They call this catch-22 the "double bind." If a woman acts like a leader—if she is assertive or aggressive in her style—she will not be as well-liked as her male colleagues. Yet if a woman leader behaves in more feminine ways—if she uses a softer tone of voice, demonstrates more feminine behavior, is less aggressive in meetings—she is less likely to be respected.

My analysis of dozens of studies of the behavior patterns of men and women in leadership proves this point. The common theme throughout was that when women did well on traditionally masculine tasks, the preferred explanation was hard work. In other words, women got there by applying more elbow grease, more time, more "stick-to-itiveness." But when men did well? People tended to believe it was because they were more competent. In an article for *The Harvard Business Review*, authors Robin Ely, Herminia Ibarra, and Deborah Kolb make the following observation about the global nature of our predicament:

> In most cultures masculinity and leadership are closely linked: The ideal leader, like the ideal man, is decisive, assertive, and independent. In contrast, women are expected to be nice, care-taking, and unselfish. The mismatch between conventionally feminine qualities and the qualities thought necessary for leadership puts female leaders in a double bind.[12]

This leaves women with a personality problem to solve. Do we allow ourselves to be true to our tendencies as leaders, risking the respect and enjoyment of our colleagues? Or do we remain true to gender stereotypes and place our potential at risk?

In a study tellingly titled "Impossible Selves," Herminia Ibarra and Jennifer Petriglieri place in sharp relief the challenge women face as they navigate these two fronts simultaneously. "Because women are evaluated on their qualities as professionals *and* as women, they may be sanctioned for either 'acting like men,' or conforming too closely to norms for female behavior—being 'too timid' or 'lacking presence with clients'"[13] (italics mine). Many of the women examined by these authors ended up trying to live in both worlds at once. The result was a kind of self-protective crouch that worked against them. As the title of the study suggests, most women found it impossible to strike a balance that would allow them to please everyone around them while being true to themselves. A Catalyst report titled "The Double-Bind Dilemma for Women in Leadership: Damned If You Do, Doomed If You Don't" documented this double standard among senior executives in both America and Europe.[14] The authors noticed that among high-level business leaders, more stereotypically "feminine" women are often "liked but not respected . . . judged too soft, emotional, and unassertive to make tough calls"[15] and do not project the kind of presence usually required for positions of authority.

So where does this leave women who are called, gifted, and motivated to lead? According to that Catalyst report, an underlying bias against the female personality in leadership creates a series of predicaments for women to negotiate:[16]

> **Predicament #1:** Women leaders are seen as being either too soft or too aggressive.
>
> **Predicament #2:** Women must work harder to reach the same level of accomplishment as their male colleagues. Women find that their accomplishments are also fleeting; their competency must be proven over and over again.
>
> **Predicament #3:** Women must choose between being seen as competent or being likable, and some choose likability over competence just to avoid the discomfort.

On the surface, you might think I'm overstating the problem. Haven't we welcomed women into leadership and moved past all this? Good question. Take my tribe, for instance. I entered full-time ministry in 1998 believing the issue of women in ministry had been resolved in my favor. Technically, it had. In many Wesleyan denominations, women have full ordination rights and have had them for decades. We hear this and think, "That issue has been resolved. Let's move on." This mindset ignores the numerous studies proving that while an issue may appear to be resolved on paper, that doesn't mean it has been resolved in the human heart. And even if the theological barrier *is* resolved, it is just one of several barriers women leaders face. Even when a woman leads effectively in distinctively "female" styles (more collaborative, team-based approaches), these styles are seen as the exceptions and not the norms of good leadership.[17] To the extent that men continue to be equated with behaviors typical of qualified leadership, that both men and women tend to default to masculine leadership styles (i.e., more assertive) as the preference, and that women continue to have to work harder to achieve the same goals as their male counterparts (or burn out in the attempt), the challenge remains.

But What about My Amazing Pastor/Sister/Friend?

I know what you're thinking: "Yeah, but I know this woman who is knocking it out of the park, and we all think she's amazing! No one cares that she's a woman. In fact, we count that in her favor!" You'd likely be right about that. The problem with your superstar example is that most women—in fact, most people—are not superstars. Female superstars attract special notice, and they even tend to receive higher evaluations on their performance than their male counterparts. It is almost as if we are unconsciously trying to overcompensate for our fallen thinking. We love a superstar! But any female who doesn't achieve superstar status will tend to get disproportionately *lower* evaluations than her male colleagues. Your superstar pastor/sister/friend reinforces our rhetoric that we wish to live in an unbiased, pre-fall world, but her exceptionality—her rarity—also reveals the stubborn reality of post-fall prejudices.

Deborah Rhode, author of *Women and Leadership*, notes that when a few superstars make it to the top of their field, their presence creates the illusion that the glass ceiling has finally been shattered when, in fact, it hasn't. And when superstars burn out or disappear from the stage, their disappearance is noticeable and attracts notice and "reinforce(s) stereotypes about women's inferior capabilities and commitment."[18] You get the point, right? In our desire to lift up a few exceptional women leaders, we can't ignore the mountain of statistical evidence stacked up against a world of competent women whose "sin" is doing good work but not breaking out of the pack.

Sallie Krawchek was one of these superstars. Her talents earned her CEO status at Merrill Lynch, Smith Barney, US Trust, the Citi Private Bank, and Sanford C. Bernstein. She was named the seventh most powerful woman in the world by *Forbes*. Krawchek is a superstar's superstar. But she learned the hard way that inside boardrooms and corner offices, even a superstar performance from a woman is harshly critiqued. When a national financial crisis surfaced in the early 2000s and the rubber hit the road, a more masculine leadership style pushed its way into her boardroom, and she was pushed out. Krawchek is convinced that this was a loss, not only for her but for the country. What was missing in that crisis, she believes, was diversity of opinion and more collaborative problem-solving—in other words, the voices and leadership styles preferred by women.[19] She argues that a healthier view of gender diversity in the leadership of organizations and a more aggressive approach toward normalizing female leaders could have helped the country avert that financial crisis. Krawchek left a lucrative career in executive leadership to become an advocate for women leaders because she believes the barriers to women's leadership have far-reaching effects. She now leads a support network that has grown to include 125,000 women. According to Ellevate, "Sallie Krawcheck's professional mission is to help women reach their financial and professional goals (or, put more bluntly, to get more money into the hands of women)."[20]

Everything we see happening to women who lead in the business world also happens to women who lead in the church. The challenge or barrier often first shows up in a woman's ability to develop trust early on in her role as pastor of a church. It shows up in a ministry leader's ability to recruit teams of qualified leaders.[21] It shows up in a church planter's ability to attract people to her young congregation. It shows up in a small group leader's interior sense of confidence. What is most maddening is that neither the woman leader nor the people she leads may be fully aware of the subtle, unconscious pressure being applied against all of them by this fallen world. The effect on those being served is a tentative acceptance of female leadership. The effect on women leaders themselves is an ongoing, inner tension. Think about what it feels like to have your authority questioned, frequently and in nonverbal ways. Think about what it feels like to walk into a room feeling suspicious of the supportiveness of folks you want to work with. Think about what it feels like to work longer hours to achieve the same goals as your male colleagues. It is difficult to form your identity as a leader when you are constantly trying to figure out how to live into the authority given to you while people around you are questioning your place.

Self-Image: How We See Ourselves

One of my favorite sayings is, "The internals impact the externals." What we think about ourselves impacts how we act and how others perceive us. But internals and externals inspire a chicken-and-egg question: does our low self-esteem feed the negative perceptions others may have of us, or do we have low self-esteem because of the negative perceptions of others? The answer—wait for it—is, "yes." Self-image and outside perception feed on one another. If we're already struggling with a negative sense of self when we step into leadership, we'll suffer for it. But even if we enter the leadership arena with a healthy self-image, we may find our sense of self threatened by the negative tide of opinion—a tide often unacknowledged and often occurring because folks around us simply don't see what they don't see. Eventually, the pressure wears on us as we internalize the negativity and allow it to manifest as self-protectiveness or lower self-esteem, neither of which rests very well on a leader.[22]

It begins with little things. Women might interact less in mixed groups or notice themselves being interrupted more often. In her TED talk about women in leadership,[23] Sheryl Sandberg (billionaire philanthropist, Facebook and Google executive, chief of staff for the US Secretary of the Treasury) quotes several studies related to the assertiveness of women highlighting that they do strange things when they lack confidence. For instance, in conversation, women tend to downplay their strengths and underestimate their contributions, while men will likely exaggerate theirs. On accepting a first job, men are more likely to negotiate higher salaries while women are much less likely to do so, at the rate of 57 percent for men to 7 percent for women. That's a striking difference in both confidence and skill at negotiating.

Does any of this matter when it comes to leading others? "Boy, it matters a lot," Sandberg says. "Because no one gets to the corner office by sitting on the side, not at the table, and no one gets the promotion if they don't think they deserve their success, or they don't even understand their own success."[24] The goal for a ministry leader, of course, is not achieving a corner office. But a woman's confidence in who she is affects her potential to succeed at her call.

In her research into the way dominant representations of gender may threaten girls' identities, psychologist Glynis Breakwell argues that social constructs feed into our sense of identity.[25] Think about how it strikes us when a man walks into a roomful of people and announces he is a pastor. We may not have any conscious thought about this at all, other than possibly an internal sense of respect for the fact that he is clergy. And he likely doesn't assume any unspoken resistance to his presence in the room. Contrast that with how we might feel when a woman walks into the same roomful of people and makes the same announcement about being a pastor. Some interest inside us is likely piqued. Depending on our theological bent, we might have *some* nonverbal resistance. But the woman? In a roomful of strangers, she is aware of the diversity of opinions about her role, but she has no idea who in that room is for her and who is against her. So how does she "present" herself? Well, she might say less or let it ride when others make comments about marriage, leadership roles, or women in the workplace. She will learn to laugh when others laugh, even at her expense, and to be patient with peoples' questions about her vocation.

I know this happens, and I know how it feels because I've been there more times than I can count. I've been invited to pastor appreciation breakfasts at the local Christian school, to community prayer events, and into more congregations than I can count where I've been the first female preacher in their pulpits. I've wondered, walking in, what all the male pastors are thinking, and sometimes I haven't had to wonder for long. I've been told straight up over eggs and grits that women don't belong in church leadership. Once, when he was trying to donate a car to a nonprofit, my husband was reprimanded for letting me preach. I've learned, in those moments, to smile and not make a scene. I've coached young women navigating those same scenarios and perceptions. I can sit at this desk and know what I know about women in spiritual leadership, but when you pile up several decades of moments, mindsets, and mumblings, that burden grows heavy. It creates a sense of self-doubt that may not prevent a woman from taking up her call, but that same self-doubt will often cause her to negatively translate those questionable moments and assume her leadership is being questioned.[26] She may find herself "apologizing her way into the room," to quote a colleague who works in the area of church development. Or "feeling her sea legs" when she stands to speak. Or becoming bitter or suspicious toward her own people.

Many women think they can just slough off the awkward moments, but it isn't that easy. When we don't deal directly with the subtle and not-so-subtle hits, they settle into the recesses of our lives. Carol Gilligan explains how this can be heard even in our physical voice. A voice connected with positive and affirming thoughts differs from one that blocks those thoughts.[27] Self-image determines influence because it drives self-presentation, and self-presentation plays a huge role in the influence leaders have over others. Think of preaching or staff leadership. Think of counseling. And think about all the times you privately (within yourself) critiqued the voice of a woman, assessing her as "angry" or "defensive" or "timid" or "shy" or her voice as too high or too low or somehow grating. Now ask yourself why. It could just be her. It could just be you. Or it could be that the combination of your internal critique and her intuitive ability to perceive it has created a toxic combination.

R. M. Arkin calls this "self-handicapping,"[28] and Blake Ashforth and Glen Kreiner discuss this effect in some detail in their work on the impact of self-image in leadership. What they've noticed is that people are prone to seeing themselves the way other people see them, blowing the old "sticks and stones" adage out of the water. Negative words, opinions, and postures *do* in fact hurt not only our sense of self but our ability to lead.[29] This effect isn't limited to women, of course. Anyone who is regularly challenged is likely to get worn out by it. We become less assertive, less confident, less attractive as a leader—and more prone to a defensive posture that puts others at odds with us. When we begin to see ourselves as victims—unheard and unappreciated—we betray our own realities. We find ourselves using all our mental energy to build a case, and before long, any argument will do. We're no longer able to see the world as it is. We become self-justifying, and that defensive posture has the opposite effect of what we intend. Nobody wants to be around someone who is chronically self-protective. Now we've created a miserable and frustrating cycle that's doomed to rewind and replay until we get fired, everyone else leaves, or we get desperate enough to seek healing.

As it turns out, what you believe about yourself matters, and a conscious choice to go after the healing of our own wounds can make a tremendous difference. A study conducted in 2001 by LeAD Labs demonstrated that women who intentionally improved their self-confidence became more effective in their careers.[30] For the women in the study, this happened by reframing challenges as opportunities so they could tackle them from a place of mental strength. The payoff is a better self-presentation. Women who portray themselves as confident, with high expectations of themselves, tend to come off as—wait for it—more competent. Our challenge is not how well we actually perform so much as how positively we are *perceived*—and not just by others but by ourselves. While this seems like a "gimme," it is a woefully unrecognized idea in conversations about women's leadership. How I see myself and my potential as a leader will impact how others see me. But here's the real irony: before I can think *positively* about myself as a leader, I have to think *realistically*.

Optimism Bias: When We Perceive "Too Good" as True

Full disclosure: I learned all this stuff the hard way. I have experienced a lifetime of defensive postures and tentative leadership. I have learned how to sell myself and my ministry just to survive. That's why I should have seen that same "sell" in the women leaders I interviewed for my doctoral project. But I missed it, and that's a story I want to tell you.

My goal for the project was to interview and survey fifty female pastors and church planters to analyze their experiences and expose commonalities between them. By the time the surveys went out, I'd already done enough research to know intellectually what I also knew experientially: gender bias is real. Hundreds of business and psychological studies can't be wrong; women face barriers. So imagine my surprise when nearly every woman church planter I surveyed came across as upbeat and complaint-free in the written portion of our interaction. They said nothing about pushback from their congregations. They were silent about conflicts with leadership teams. They barely mentioned financial difficulties. It didn't add up. What was I missing?

I scrubbed my notes for answers and discovered a study by social psychologist Faye Crosby, who stumbled on a surprising phenomenon. Most women, she found, are unaware of having been victims of subtle gender discrimination. In fact, they tend to deny it even when it is objectively true and when they see that women in general experience it.[31] Like I said, even though I was aware that I had conditioned myself to be optimistic, this was still a stunning find. It led me down a rabbit hole investigating something called optimism bias.

Optimism bias, or unrealistic optimism, is defined as "a favorable difference between the risk estimate a person makes for himself or herself and the risk estimate suggested by a relevant, objective standard."[32] An early and helpful work in this field of study is *The Optimism Bias: Why We're Wired to Look on the Bright Side* by Tali Sharot.[33] Sharot is a psychologist who runs a "brain lab" at University College

London. Her work has been further popularized by a TED talk in which she describes in layman's terms the positive and negative effects of optimism bias on people and cultures.[34] Sharot explains that roughly 80 percent of people are optimistic, a trait that leads to a greater sense of well-being and a decrease in anxiety and stress. Other researchers suggest the same—that an optimistic disposition in general leads to a stronger ability to persevere through trials and an increased sense of hope.[35]

This is all good and healthy, right? But a general sense of optimism is not the same as *unrealistic* optimism. Those with unrealistic optimism tend to see their own futures as more positive than statistically probable.[36] This attitude leads them to make decisions based on what statistical probability suggests will be an unrealistic future. Apply this dynamic to a woman on her way to a leadership role, and it quickly becomes a recipe for failure. Believing herself to be invincible, she plows ahead with her dreams without proper assessment, mentors, or tools for the work. She convinces herself everything is just fine until the day it all comes crashing down around her, either in the form of her own emotional crash or that of the house of cards she has built.

This, as it turns out, was the more accurate story beneath the optimism of those initial surveys of church planters. Once I discovered the phenomenon of optimism bias, I was able to enter into personal interviews with better questions. I gave women room to talk, and the stories I heard made my own challenges seem mild by comparison. I'll spare you the worst of their stories but share this comment from one rather successful planter: "I was invited to speak as a church planter at an annual conference a year ago. The guys got up and said, 'It has been awesome and I have five hundred (members),' and I got up and said, 'This is the hardest thing I've ever done and it has been miserable and it has been tough.'" When questioned about the dissonance between her survey answers and the overall tone of her interview, she said, "The only way to survive as a female church planter is to know how to sell yourself so people will invest in you." She had become so accustomed to selling herself that answering a survey optimistically was second nature to her. As another woman put it, "We don't want to show a weakness. We are conditioned that everything has to be perfect. Your house has to be clean, your kids have to be well-fed. We don't realize the toll that takes on our psyche. We don't even realize it."[37]

Women face barriers, and when women deny that, they are denying a reality that could alter their professional trajectory. I'll say it again: a general disposition of optimism is a wonderful posture to take when pursuing a new work. Admirable, even. But blind optimism—a self-protective bias toward only the good without an ability to acknowledge what truly *is*—will work against a leader by preventing her from acknowledging the warning signs of failure or from seeking the information and support needed to create a sustainable ministry over time.

This is why I'm passionate about simply acknowledging what is real. It can be a game-changer. When I can accept my own giftedness, do the research, acknowledge the challenges, and take authority over the position given me, I can more confidently reach for leadership roles for which I'm qualified, and I can be more proactive in getting the support I need to become everything I'm created to be.

Kingdom Vision: How Jesus Sees Us

Some of the most beautiful scenes between men and women in the Bible happen when Jesus is around. Maybe the best one is the scene when Jesus is in the home of a religious leader for dinner (Luke 7:36–50). A woman with a questionable reputation shows up at the house while they are eating and, standing at Jesus's feet, begins to weep. Her tears fall on his feet. Having nothing else to work with, she begins to wipe away the tears with her hair. Kneeling there on the floor, her head close to his feet, she begins to kiss the feet of Jesus and massage them with oil. In this sacramental act, she joins the fellowship of biblical women who dared to walk back across the line of Genesis 3 into the garden of Eden.

Of course, everyone in the house is scandalized—except Jesus. He treasures this moment. He doesn't want anyone to miss it. He turns to the room and to the people who are already asking how this can be, and asks, "Do you see this woman?" It is a profound and telling question. Did anyone in that roomful of men acknowledge her humanity? Jesus wants them to respect the statement she has made. Even more, he wants to honor how she relates to him. The obvious contrast is with Jesus's host, Simon, who has neglected some basic principles of first-century hospitality. But Jesus doesn't compare people. He compares *faith*.

Don't miss the point. This moment isn't about how Simon sees the woman. It is about how Simon sees *Jesus*. In this scene, Jesus begins to put the pieces of Genesis 1 back together. He partners with another human being (one who happens to be female) to teach Simon that how he relates to God determines how he sees the world. One who sees Jesus clearly will also see those around him clearly, and one who honors Jesus will also honor women. In other words, when I am rightly related to God, I will rightly relate to his creation.

Do you see her?

It is a powerful question, isn't it? Jesus's recognition and respect for the women in his presence affirms that humans have bodies and stories and spiritual gifts that are designed to be in partnership with God to build the kingdom on earth. Do you remember what Bill Gates said to that roomful of Saudi businessmen? "Well, if you're not fully utilizing half the talent in the country, you're not going to get too close to the top ten."[38] He's right, and that translates. If we are not rightly relating to half the Christian community, we are not going to get close to the kingdom of God. Male and female are partnered in the work of realizing God's kingdom on earth. In some obvious ways, the genders complement one another, but in all ways, they are in partnership. Body and soul, character and ministry, gifts and call are all interwoven. Together, we are designed to lead all creation back to God. How we perceive that challenge—and each other—makes all the difference.

CHAPTER 3

RESOURCES AND BENCHMARKS

Show Me the Numbers

In the classic chicken-and-egg conundrum, sometimes the right answer is "yes." Take, for instance, the question of which comes first when it comes to funding and resources for ministry. Do resources follow effectiveness or is effectiveness increased when a ministry is properly resourced? The answer in most cases is *yes.*

I remember the day our denominational church development director called to let me know they'd received a bit of a windfall after the sale of a church building in our district. The funds from that sale were designated for new projects in our area, and while the church I'd planted was now several years old, it still fell into the "new project" category. Two other churches, both started within a year of ours, were also being considered as beneficiaries of those funds.

"So you don't hear it from someone else," the director

said when he called, "I want to be the one to tell you that we've decided to give the proceeds of that sale to Paul's (not his real name) church." He went on to explain that since Paul's church was growing rapidly, they needed the funds for physical expansion. It was the right thing to do for them, the director said.

And he was right. It *was* the right thing—*if* the litmus test was attendance. Paul's church had broken out of the pack of new church start-ups in our area and was doing great. His church was growing rapidly; from all indications, it was healthy and would make it for the long haul. From a strictly personal perspective, I had nothing but enthusiasm for Paul's ministry. He was a good friend. We'd coached each other along in the early days (his church was planted within six months of mine). I considered him a faithful leader. His ministry was solid. I wanted nothing but the best for Paul and his church. I also understood that there are only so many dollars to go around and, if numbers were the bottom line in that decision, then a rapidly growing, highly attended church was a more efficient use of funds.

I got it. I still get it. After all, I'm a church leader. I know what matters.

Because I get it, I need to pause here and tell you that I hesitated to share this story with you. I don't want to lend to the suspicion that I approach any of this as a victim. But I can hear you now, dear reader. "*Aha!*" you're saying, "I knew she was an angry female! I *knew* there was more to this book than kingdom advancement!"

At least, that's what I'd be saying if I were in your chair.

Now that we've acknowledged what this story might

sound like, we also need to acknowledge what is true. The fact was Paul's church had consistently received more support than ours. His church originated from a sponsoring "mother church" while ours was an unparented "parachute drop." He was fearless when it came to asking for what he needed from the denomination to which we both belonged. He seemed to come to those conversations as an insider while I always felt more like an outsider. I was always more timid when it came to the "ask." And he had a strong base of leaders from day one, including several business owners on his team, who helped him learn to negotiate for what was required to grow an organization. He had a strong mentor and advocate in the form of a layperson with a passion for evangelism. While we both felt a lot of pressure to conform to the expectations set for our respective projects, Paul seemed to have more resources from the outset to meet and even exceed those expectations.

Meanwhile, our church never seemed quite able to catch a strong wind. We lacked seasoned leadership—people with business acumen, for example—on our team. We struggled to gain momentum to build critical mass in our Sunday worship services. Meanwhile, I struggled to find mentors and coaches who understood our particular dynamics. More than once, in fact, professional coaches told me they didn't coach women and wished me well on my quest to find the right coach (I'm still looking). Yet for all those barriers in the way of a strong start, the benchmarks for success set by denominational officials were the same for my church as for those of my male colleagues. We were given the same deadline to be a self-sustaining church, with no "give" on that expectation.

The denomination in which I was raised has been ordaining women for fifty years, but in our haste to affirm the role of women in ministry, we have missed recognizing the more nuanced challenges of female leadership. It is as if, now that we have blessed women to lead and have encouraged churches to receive their leadership, we have done our part. This is not only true of the denomination in which I was raised or even of pastors in general. Across the board, in both sacred and secular settings, there remains a kind of naïve misunderstanding of the complexities that accompany female leadership. We lack understanding about how female-led organizations grow and what is needed to help them succeed. Embedded in the choice to encourage female leadership is a multitude of resulting issues still waiting to be addressed in order for that leadership to be effective:

- How do financial resources play into the big picture?
- How do women use mentors and coaches, and where are the coaches they need?
- What about practical resources to equip women leaders, like training in the art of negotiation and networking?
- Where are training opportunities that address women's leadership styles?
- Who will teach us how to attract and raise up solid leaders?
- Who will show us how (and why) to bargain for better salaries?
- How do women leaders find the resources they need to succeed in a vocation that is demanding for even the best trained among us?

Once we've answered the question of whether or not women *should* lead—yes, they should!—now we must learn what happens when women *do* lead so we can be "shrewd as snakes and innocent as doves" (Matt. 10:16, my paraphrase) in the work of sending female leaders into a world that may not understand them.

Roxanne Stone, editor in chief at Barna Group, made this same observation at the conclusion of Barna's 2017 study on the state of pastors in the US:

> With nearly half of the paid workforce now made up of women, it might seem as though the job is done . . . But there are still significant growing pains on the journey toward gender parity. For most women, these are less about representation in the workplace and more about expectations and fair treatment. In our research, women point out inequality in promotions and in pay. While the American public may be comfortable with women in senior leadership positions, the facts are that women are still under-represented in executive suites and paid less than men for the same jobs.[1]

As it turns out, the work of raising up strong women leaders is "chicken and egg" work—affirmation *and* resources, giftedness *and* equipping, equality *and* understanding. It begins, as we've said already, with acknowledging what *is*. Certainly, there is a place to acknowledge trauma, but we are not victims. We are people living in a fallen world on a journey toward kingdom advancement. With that mindset, let's take a look at some of the more common barriers to resources that women leaders encounter.

Mentors and Coaches

Let's begin with what it takes to find the right voice to coach a female leader. Since women comprise a small piece of the total market of ministry leaders and pastors, we can't blame coaches and trainers for going where the market dictates. Materials and training opportunities are geared toward the majority audience, and women are not in the majority. In the church world, women comprise less than 10 percent of the total market of pastors in senior positions and an estimated 5 percent of church planters.[2] Let's compare these percentages with the 8.2 percent of women CEOs at Fortune 500 companies (as of this writing), just so we can acknowledge that the world in general is not breaking any records when it comes to placing women in leadership roles.[3]

What this means is that women often step into leadership without access to the kind of individualized coaching and training that makes the difference between good and great leadership. As the experts tell us, "Aspiring leaders need role models whose styles and behaviors they can experiment with and evaluate according to their own standards and others' reactions. Fewer female leaders means fewer role models and can suggest to young would-be leaders that being a woman is a liability."[4]

The paucity of women role models, mentors, and coaches has been a constant across several decades. Studies show that women tend to be less likely than men to find or use a mentor. A 1991 survey of 229 women and 281 men discovered that "gender was significantly related" to a woman's lack of access to a mentor.[5] Nearly ten years later, Richard Nemanick, author and expert in mentoring for leaders, found in his study that even informal mentoring relationships seemed more difficult for professional women to attain.[6] In 2011, the professional networking website LinkedIn conducted a similar survey of a thousand female leaders and discovered we had still not made much progress. Nicole Williams, LinkedIn's career expert at the time, wrote, "We were curious whether women really are having a distinct experience [with mentors]. So we found two different surveys that confirmed that, in fact, men are more likely to get workplace guidance than women. They're more likely to have a mentor. They're more likely to be asked to be a mentor. They're more likely to have asked someone to be a mentor."[7] In an NPR interview about the LinkedIn study, Williams mentioned that "women have that 'got-it-all-together' disease."[8] In other words, women have become so used to advocating for themselves and working hard to make it all work that they've forgotten how to approach work as learners. A *Harvard Business Review* report stated, "Women believe that hard work alone will be enough, that hard work and long hours, not connections, account for their advancement."[9] These perceptions are not just internally felt. In Barna's research on what Americans think about women in power, women were more likely to report that they felt the external pressure of an expectation of perfection—a sense that they were responsible for everything and everyone.[10]

And all the women in the room said, "Amen."

With enough internal and external pressure, it is almost as if we've lost our will to seek out mentors. In my own less formal survey of women church planters, I discovered that most had used a coach at some point, but among those who had not, about half said it was because they hadn't found the right person, or because they hadn't been encouraged to seek out a coach. Some said they simply couldn't afford it. One woman summed up many of the comments I heard: "Sometimes you just feel like you're all by yourself."[11] In an all-by-yourself world, meeting even one more expectation can require more energy than a person has.

Then, of course, there are the perception issues that crop up when women are mentored by men. Even though many men are not only capable of mentoring or coaching women but may even be the best coaches for high-functioning female leaders, multiple studies confirm that most men don't want to be seen as being inappropriately associated with women (I don't think we needed a study to tell us that). So, more often than not, they choose not to be available. Also, women are less likely to ask a man to be a mentor, even if he might be more effective than another woman at coaching her in the skills she needs. How often are we shuffling a marvelously gifted young woman off to another female who happens to have free time and a desire to help, rather than setting her up with the man (or woman) who can fully challenge her vocationally? Herminia Ibarra and her colleagues have discovered that many women don't end up fulfilling their potential as leaders not because they aren't mentored, but because they aren't mentored *well*. They end up with mentors who are the right gender but who possess the wrong skill set or who don't have enough clout.[12] In that equation, everyone suffers. How much potential are we leaving on the table, when the right action is to expect both men and women to be whole enough to interact in healthy ways? These are questions worth exploring.

Training

What about training? It isn't just individualized guidance that leaders need, but best practices. In a study of female MBA students, Susan Vinnicombe (who has written and researched extensively on the topic of women in leadership) and Val Singh (a researcher and professor who specializes in diversity on corporate boards) discovered that women are hungry for the kind of training that takes their unique circumstances into account. They noticed that many MBA programs miss the mark when it comes to filling gaps women experience when they are enrolled in the programs. They also cite a Catalyst survey of 1,684 MBA students from twelve universities. Half the students in the study were female. When asked what would make a difference in their experience as students, an overwhelming majority of women—90 percent—said they lacked female role models and training in line with their style of leadership.[13]

It would be easy at this point to argue that women do have access to the same training opportunities as men. Even if many church networks (like Acts 29 or the Summit Network) are geared toward men, women can still attend their conferences and seminars. You might wonder, is it too much to ask for women to go after the resources they need to get the job done, even if it means being a minority in the room? I'd respond, no, it is not too much to ask, *if* those conferences and seminars had women's leadership styles in mind. For instance, women tend to be more collaborative in nature, and often, women have different gaps in knowledge from their male colleagues or different challenges to focus on. I can't remember taking a single seminary class or continuing education opportunity that focused on financial management, the art of negotiation, or the recruitment of coaches and mentors. But research tells us these are clearly the needs. One denominational official explained, "I find that [women leaders] are very prepared theologically, they are good teachers . . . where they need help is the leadership part, recruiting the . . . team." Another official concurred, saying, "I think leadership training is definitely what we need. Another area is in coaching. I think I only know two or three women coaches; it is hard to find really good women coaches." The church's leaders—*all kinds* of leaders—are starving for high-quality training and for coaches who will also require training.

Finances

Finances are another area where we limit the resources directed at women who lead, particularly those in key leadership positions. I don't want to narrow our conversation only to the experience of pastors, but I also don't want to miss this opportunity to make a point. If a significant percentage of the Christian world does not affirm the role of women in spiritual leadership, then it stands to reason that the same percentage would be reluctant to attend or give to churches led by women. This means that women fish from a smaller pond from the outset. Maybe Americans have acclimated to the presence of female leadership at work and in politics, but in the church? Not so much.[14] One woman pastor said, with no apology but a lot of resolve, "My inability to draw and sustain a crowd . . . correlates to the giving needed to sustain a worshipping community." She's right. You can't get funding from people who aren't there.

One moral of my earlier story about my friend Paul the church planter was that in a world of limited dollars, the rapid-growth, high-attendance churches win. Boards, agencies, and foundations with funds to share find themselves making choices that are unintentionally gender-biased. Sometimes, the choices are not only intentional but unapologetically so. One clergywoman reported being told by a denominational official, "There is little evidence supporting the idea that women can successfully plant churches, so we are not willing to put any money into it." These kinds of comments aren't the sole property of conservative tribes. "I don't think [my denomination] in general wants to invest in female church planters," an official once told me. "I had a church developer from the Midwest call me and say, 'We had this woman test well on everything and she looks like she'd be a good planter, but she is a woman and a mom, so I was told to call you and ask if we should give her a chance.' And I was like, why on earth would you not give her a chance? I think the denomination struggles."

Another ministry leader said that without adequate financial support, she was left to create her own faith-stretching way through. "It is totally God who has been involved with this. I received no pay for many, many years. Just told that I was supposed to preach the Word of God, and whoever showed up, showed up." Yet another woman, tapped to develop a new church, said, "They gave me an impossible task as the first female planter [in my area] with no resources and no people and no support." She suspects her superiors intentionally set her up for failure.

Subtle dynamics are in play when women lead. Women often attract a less financially secure crowd, many of whom are coming to Christ for the first time. One leader said,

"[Our ministry] serves persons in poverty. Our average tithe is twenty-three dollars per week." She reported that her denomination recognized her work but failed to provide the financial resources to help it flourish. "The [denomination] wanted to see if we would survive before offering any monetary funds. So my husband and I are the ones who had to put the funds in. However, we have learned to live on very little and even had to ask other denominations to help." Another leader observed, "We are dealing with people who have either been hurt by a church or 'unchurched,' for lack of a better term. They don't understand discipleship, or they ask, 'Where is my money going? I want to see what I've purchased.' [I've had to] operate on a rubber-band, bubble-gum type of budget. God has gotten us through hard times. We've never been in the red, but I think that's the biggest challenge. [It] is getting people, especially now, when the economy is hurting."

I can hear you saying (justifiably), "Yeah, but male pastors fight for every dollar, too." Absolutely. Yes. They don't call us nonprofits for nothing. The point is not that one gender has it easy while another suffers, but that for all the difficulty that goes with church funding, women have even fewer resources at their disposal. In their study of the challenges faced by women in leadership, Robin Ely and Deborah Rhode note that women often have difficulty accessing the same information as their male colleagues.[15] Men in general have greater access to inner circles of support. "Women in traditionally male-dominated settings often have difficulty breaking into the 'old boys' loop of advice and professional development opportunities."[16]

I'm not a golfer, but many women are. Still, women who do golf are obviously less likely to be with "the guys" on the golf course when an opportunity arises for a conversation about a major donation toward a building campaign. Men have ways of talking with each other that don't fit the culture of cross-gender conversations. Also, women may have less access to conversations outside of business hours or on trips. They are less likely to negotiate funding or salaries.[17] All these differences show up in frustrated leaders. One comment summed up the feelings of many: "I am not a natural fundraiser; I avoid the 'ask.'"

All these feelings that show up in stark relief for female pastors also present in various shades for women in leadership roles across the board. Even in areas where women leaders are affirmed, such as youth ministry or nonprofit ministry leadership, there are differences that will require patience and courage.

Congregational Leaders

Then there is the challenge of gathering and training effective lay leaders for the work of ministry. Again, this is not the sole problem of women leaders, but with a smaller pool to draw from and multiple factors in play (like the tendency of strong men to resist the leadership of women or the lack of adequate funds to hire gifted women leaders), establishing qualified team members is a significant issue for women. One leader told me, "The most difficult thing is keeping [leaders] around. We lost eleven staff in the last twelve months with the merger . . . it's hard when you invest that much time in someone, and you know it's best if they step down but you're trying to cultivate other leaders and rebuilding that trust with them . . . just finding the right people at the right time." A perceptive leader diagnosed her issue in this way:

> It took me a while to figure out that, when you're reaching the unchurched and the de-churched and the never churched, they are not confident to lead. They don't feel equipped. They don't think they know the Bible, and they don't, but I always felt like you learn as you teach, right? So it took me a while to figure out that none of those people felt ready. They were super excited, and they would do anything I asked. But the leading part was really, really hard. I'm four years down the line, and it took three years to move my folks from attenders to leaders. You have to invest in them for three full years before they are ready to assume responsibility for their own place in ministry.

When we set barrier on top of barrier, it is hard to ignore the cumulative evidence. It isn't that men don't also deal with challenges, but scores of studies reveal that women have a steeper hill to climb when taking on the leadership of an organization or church. About 40 percent of women in business and political leadership believe they have to work harder or more than their male colleagues.[18] Further, women report having to achieve higher standards and develop a more tailored set of management skills in order to compete with men.[19] Let's talk about those higher standards.

Benchmarks for Success

With benchmarks, women face a "damned if you do, damned if you don't" situation. About half the women surveyed in one study said that the "major reason more women are not in top leadership positions in business is that women are held to higher standards and have to do more to prove themselves."[20] About a third of men hold that same view. But even if they're not held to a higher standard, women find themselves having to climb a steeper hill just to get to the same summit. Thus, gender-neutral benchmarks are more easily reached by men, who are unencumbered by the obstacles faced by women. When I think about this, I get a mental image of Egypt's pharaoh, who first made all the Israelite slaves make bricks from straw. He gave them a daily quota that kept them working from morning till night. When he became more nervous about how quickly they were multiplying, he demanded they make the same number of bricks without any supply of straw. They'd have to go find their own but would be punished if they weren't still producing at the expected level.[21]

It's a somewhat pale reflection of Pharaoh's Egypt, but male leaders make their quota of bricks with their straw provided, while women leaders have the same quota but must gather straw on their own. In our haste to promote equality, we're simply not taking into account the extra challenges women face. Women are measured by the same yardstick as their male colleagues and punished by that same yardstick. Inside Christian ministries, especially, we're asking women to compete within a system that wasn't built with them in mind. If benchmarks are aggressively geared toward a rapid growth model, and if expectations are set based on the standards of a male-dominated culture, women will not be able to compete for limited resources.

If we roll up all of the above, here's what we discover. Women spiritual leaders are being asked to work harder, with fewer resources at their disposal, to reach unrealistic goals based on the standards of a male-dominated culture. The common result for many women is frustration and burnout, as well as the proliferation of skewed beliefs among both men and women about women's ability to lead and lead well.

Is there some great leveler that evens the playing field? Or are women doomed to either work twice as hard or lag behind in this fallen world?

God Is Not Broke

Some of my best lessons have been learned from colleagues in Africa who experience the daily call to follow Jesus in a challenging environment. A Nigerian pastor and seminary professor, who lives on the edge between the Muslim-dominated north and threatened Christians in the south, vividly described for me life on the front lines of the spiritual battle being waged over the souls in his country.

I was stunned when he told me—in the same tone of voice Americans use to talk about going to the grocery store—that in his part of the world, "We wake up every day prepared to die." He could talk with great seriousness about his country's situation and yet still display such joy when we worshipped together while on mission in another country. In a little chapel in southeast Asia, he led us in an African chant that I believe ought to become the anthem of every serious follower of Jesus:

I must go with Jesus anywhere, anywhere,
no matter the roughness of the road.
I must go! I must go!

My friend led us around, dancing in a circle, singing that song so joyfully, so hopefully, all of us began clapping our hands as if rough roads were a great thing to be on. And in fact, they are, because those are precisely the roads that lead us toward the kingdom of God.

Another colleague is a professor at a seminary in Liberia. Recently, he told me the story of how he came to be a pastor. He said he'd had the call for years but ran from it. He didn't want to be a pastor because he had a college degree and was marketable. "Money can weigh heavily on an African's decision to follow Jesus," he said. "There is no money in becoming a pastor. You will be poor your whole life and have no way to take care of yourself in your old age." Then, smiling, he went on, "But God kept after me."

During Liberia's civil war in the 1990s, this friend told me that, in an effort to save his still unsurrendered life, he found himself fleeing from one town to another with all he had to his name in the one bag he carried. When he was stopped at a security point, mistaken for a rebel by a guard, he was sure he'd be killed. They forced him, at gunpoint, to remove all his clothes. There he was, with his bag in his hand, standing before the guards in his underwear with a gun to his head.

He assumed it was his last moment alive, but then they told him to run. He did. "While I was running," he said, "I realized the only reason I was still alive was because God had a purpose for me. Right then, while I was running, I committed my life to him and have served him ever since. I have no retirement fund and no way of taking care of myself in my old age. And you know? That used to scare me, but then one day, I realized, 'God is not broke!'"

Listening to my Liberian brother tell this story, I thought

again about my friend in Nigeria, dancing in a circle with strangers in a remote corner of the world. "I must go with Jesus anywhere, anywhere, no matter the roughness of the road. I must go! I must go!"

These men stand in the spiritual company of those disciples in Luke 9, who were told by Jesus himself to go out into towns and villages armed with nothing but the gospel. "Take nothing for the journey," Jesus told them.[22] Why? Because God is not broke. Because Jesus all by himself is not only worth everything, but when Jesus commands us to go, he gives us power and authority enough to cover all needs.

Jesus is enough, even when the road is rough.

Take nothing. This is so counterintuitive, and so *not us.*

"Take nothing for the journey," Jesus advises, while we strategize our self-sufficiencies. This is a hard message to incorporate into our current reality. We want to say, "Yes, but that was not this."

Unless it is . . . because spiritual principles are meant to transfer, which means that even if the circumstances change, the principles still work. In this case, "Take nothing" is code for, "Unless you're traveling with the power and authority of the Holy Spirit, nothing else matters." In the context of a supernatural worldview, it means believing that your nothing or not-enough is everything in the hands of an almighty God, who has more to offer through your empty hands than he does through your full ones. What we hoard is temporary, but what God sends through us is eternal.

Given enough statistics, studies, and stories, we could easily be left feeling as if women have no chance in this lopsided economy of resources. But the hope at the end of this chapter is that God is not broke. The spiritual resources that matter are not being dispensed with an eyedropper by some miserly guy who is afraid he may run out at any moment. We serve a God who owns the cattle on a thousand hills;[23] who knows us, sees us, and gifts us lavishly. I'm living proof. Our church may not have gotten a share of that denominational grant mentioned at the beginning of this chapter, but we survived that season, and we've survived a dozen more since. We've more than survived. Today, we are a thriving missional community.

God is not broke. Though we may find ourselves scraping for resources, though the work can be so challenging at times that we feel like we're always waking up "prepared to die," God stands ready to fill us with all we need. Luke phrases God's intentions well: "If you then, who are evil, know how to give good gifts to your children, how much more will the heavenly Father give the Holy Spirit to those who ask him!" (Luke 11:13 ESV). Our God is a giver of every good gift, which means that Jesus's "Take nothing for the journey" is not a call to be careless about resources but a reminder that even when we feel like we have nothing to bring to this work we've been given, our God has our back. That's a promise.

CHAPTER 4

THE PASTORAL CARE BARRIER

She Loves Me, Yeah, Yeah, Yeah

In the early days of the COVID-19 pandemic, when being out in the world seemed so dangerous, I found myself wildly protective of my flock. In the absence of weekly worship, I wanted my people to know I was still there. I was most concerned that no one feel left behind or left out, so I worked double-time. I made phone calls, sent texts, created special emails and videos, even visited and shared Communion in driveways. I was particularly protective of those in our church who were single, lonely, prone to addiction, or otherwise isolated by the virus. I am glad about all the tangible ways we reached out; they were reasonable and compassionate approaches to pastoral care in that extraordinary season.

Yet, like most ministry leaders, I knew I couldn't sustain that pace and level of activity forever. As the global crisis wore on, I found myself struggling between feeling the responsibility to be personally involved in as many lives as possible and letting our folks care organically for each other. Most of the time, the former option won. Pandemic life held tremendous sway over my maternal instincts. I was protective, mothering, emotional—and people felt it. I can't count the number of times during that season when folks in my spiritual care sincerely and gratefully uttered some version of, "You've been our rock," or, "You were like a mother to all of us." I felt validated by their kind words. The affirmation stoked the fires and made me want to do more—until I couldn't anymore. Eventually, like so many others in my circumstance, I burned out, and then I checked out. I simply stopped reaching out, and in the absence of another system, folks were left to fend for themselves. Thankfully, I had good and understanding people around me, but I could easily have been another pandemic statistic (a Barna survey found that 29 percent of pastors were "considering their options" during the pandemic[1]).

As it turns out, this impulse to care, as innocent and good as it sounds, can become a problem. An overdeveloped need to care for body and soul will not only burn out a spiritual leader but can stifle the growth of a church. When we, as spiritual leaders, place too much personal emphasis on pastoral care (and by this, I mean individualized care for persons with expressed needs) to the exclusion of healthy boundaries, we decide that loving the other is more important than Sabbath. Then we shoot past the boundary set by Jesus himself, who taught us to love our neighbor as ourselves. Enmeshment ensues, boundaries are lost, gossip abounds, and truth is ignored.

In a 2015 blog post, Carey Nieuwhof, Christian thought

leader, made the argument that a pastor whose personal time and attention is focused on congregational care will lack sufficient time, resources, or perspective to create church growth.[2] This dynamic is only heightened for women since, generally speaking, we tend to have a more nurturing, connected approach to relationships. (Yes, I get that we're stereotyping here, but stereotypes do exist for a reason. Carol Gilligan notes, "Often stereotypes and preconceptions are more powerful than facts in shaping views and influencing actions."[3]) A female leader is often seen not as a professional but as a mother figure, and as a mother, she will be held to certain standards of "ideal motherhood."[4] When she does not live up to that image, she may become the target of others' disillusionment. Whether this ought to be the case is not the issue. Gilligan notes that women tend to define themselves in terms of their relationships, "but also judge themselves in terms of their ability to care."[5]

Compare this approach with that of most men. It probably doesn't need to be said that on the whole, men and women have different approaches to intimacy. In general, men tend to develop identity first, then intimacy. For women, identity and intimacy happen simultaneously. Women tend to know themselves in relationship with and to others.[6] Think of it in terms of how we think and learn. Some of us engage more independently with information, while others tend to better absorb information when it is presented in relationship. Psychologists and educators often talk about disconnected and connected learners. In the simplest comparison, it is the difference between an engineer and an artist.

Since women tend to learn and connect relationally, that's what we assume they'll do. In other words—lean in, because this is a huge point—*when the pastor is a woman, we probably think less about "pastoral care" as merely one of her job responsibilities and more as "who she is."*[7] She is a mother, a caregiver, a nurturer. Pastoral care becomes the primary expectation rather than a piece of the professional puzzle. Never mind her job title or the church's need for systems development, staff management, or vision-casting. We want her to take care of us emotionally and *personally*. Depending on her gifts, call, and sense of self, she may acquiesce because she, too, believes that nurture is something she ought to offer selflessly.[8] It's just "who she is."

What could be a better fit? If I'm a pastor and the need is pastoral care, then aren't we good to go? If only it were that easy. The fact is, pastoral care, when left exclusively to the pastor, whether that person is male or female, as Carey Nieuwhof puts it, "simply doesn't scale."[9] When it all hinges on one frazzled person who is taking care of every soul, tending to every patient, visiting every prisoner, relating to every bride or grieving widow, not to mention counseling and praying over everyone's personal crises, it becomes impossible for that spiritual leader to do any visionary system-building, disciple-making, community-developing work. Ironically, in a stressful environment, those personal connections may create the kind of good feelings that make a person feel useful and keep her from bailing out (unless compassion is not her primary gift). Those good feelings are more than just emotions. Simon Sinek, an author and speaker on issues related to leadership, writes, "Our brains are wired to release oxytocin when in the presence of our tribe and cortisol, the chemical that produces the feeling of anxiety, when we feel vulnerable and alone."[10] A preference for pastoral care is perpetuated by the sheer fact that it creates a pleasant mental environment in those who are already wired for care. Why build a healthy, distributed system of care when I can do it myself and get all the good feels in the process?

Nieuwhof paints a typical scenario for ministry leaders enmeshed in prioritizing and hoarding congregational care rather than building systems that pass that care on to community members:

> You're working on your sermon or some long-term planning and your phone buzzes, letting you know that someone just got admitted to hospital or that a couple needs to see you NOW for marriage counseling. What do you do? Most leaders respond immediately to the need (because we're pastors, after all). And that leaves the sermon prep or project to the next day. Which also gets interrupted by a new crisis. Which moves your work to the evening, or the weekend, or into family time. And soon, you only write your sermons on Saturday night.
>
> Eventually, you just can't keep up. And, predictably, three things happen:
>
> - You get completely overwhelmed, and maybe even burn out.
> - The congregation gets upset with you because you're not as responsive as you used to be when the church was smaller.
> - The church stops growing, because few human beings can sustain that level of pastoral care beyond 200 attenders, and many burn out trying (see point 1).

What seemed manageable when your church was just starting or was smaller, feels completely out of control as your church pushes 150, 200, or 300 in weekend attendance.[11]

Sound familiar? I grieve the lost potential, lost Sabbaths, and lost health I and my church have sustained because I gave away too much at the altar of "pastoral care." Even writing that, I anticipate your heart-wrenching critique: "Didn't Jesus teach us to love our neighbors as ourselves? Didn't he teach us that the difference between sheep and goats is precisely at the point of our willingness to give food to the hungry, clothes to the naked, hospitality to the stranger, care for the sick and imprisoned? If pastoral care is wrong, I don't wanna be right!"

I hear you, and to a degree, you are exactly right. Now, please hear me: genuine, loving care for souls is critical to the life and health of any church. It is biblically sound and important in the development of a kingdom community. I vote for pastoral care. That's not the problem. The problem is with how we structure—or don't—to make it happen. If the only structure in place is, "When I have a personal need, I'll call the pastor/ministry leader/professional," we're doomed to create an emotionally dependent and growth-averse atmosphere. If that structure is cemented in place by an assumption that if the leader is a woman, it's what she ought to be doing anyway, then we have doomed both church and leader. The church will struggle to grow, and the leader will struggle for time and space to envision and plan strategically for that growth.

In my own surveys of women leaders, some version of

this comment from one leader was a common refrain: "One of my strongest gifts aside from starting new things and fixing broken things is pastoral care. I have to watch that I don't get so drawn into someone's issues or problems at the church that I forget I'm also the founding and lead pastor of this church and that I have to delegate to others."[12]

Edward Morgan, a pioneer in the area of pastoral ministry, puts the potential risk in stark relief: "A sort of pastoral masochism can result from an inability to say no to certain needs expressed under certain conditions by other people. The leader walks the second mile so often that her feet bleed, when this seemingly pastoral attitude may simply reinforce the dependent's dependency and prevent the steps needed for growing independence."[13] If we, as caring humans, don't learn how to master our nurturing tendencies so that they work for and not against us, we will quickly find ourselves mired in caring for individuals at the expense of the whole, not to mention the harm we inflict on ourselves (more on this later).

Now, in a spirit of full disclosure, I should tell you that all this is probably a lot easier for me to say than for someone else. After all, my pastoral care style is, "Get over it!" I deeply resonate with a Bob Newhart sketch where he promises to cure whatever ails his patients by yelling two words at them: "Stop it!"[14] I wouldn't call myself disconnected, but in any spiritual gifts inventory, shepherding consistently falls near the bottom of my list. I'm a pragmatist and an entrepreneur—a church planter with a strong pull toward missions and evangelism. I love seeing communities develop, but for my part, I want to get in, build it, and then watch it work. That's my sweet spot.[15] This means it may be easier for me than for the next leader to absorb and defend Nieuwhof's theory that excessive pastor-centered pastoral care stifles church growth. It may also be why I so deeply want women leaders to personally wrestle with this idea and get honest about how it may be affecting the potential of their leadership or congregation. The goal is not only the success of the leader, but to see the whole community serving out of a wide variety of gifts.

Of course, pastoral care *is* important, and a more nurturing leadership style has great capacity for enriching the vocation of a female leader. The trick is in exercising that gift in ways that bear much fruit. This may be exactly the place for an associate gifted to carry the stories of a congregation. It may be the perfect fit for a lay leader who is most at home when caring for souls in crisis situations. Or that same gift of care for souls may play out in more creative ways. In another chapter, we will talk at length about the value of collaboration, a particular strength of women who display a connected learning and leadership style. I would say that collaboration—team building, mentorship, consensus building—is the wave of the future as the era of "big-box/rapid-growth" churches loses steam and missional communities continue to emerge. Connected learners, natural collaborators, and strong team builders will find themselves at the forefront of this movement. So be encouraged, my nurturing friends. What you bring to the table *matters*. What we're after in this chapter is not a negative critique of pastoral care but a recognition that, left unchecked and "un-holified," this practice can stand in the way of women who want to lead well and bear fruit.

So how do strong, competent, gifted, and called women of God not get stuck in the rut of mothering every person who comes through the door? We must identify our true motives. In our practice of compassionate care, what drives us? Are we operating from a place of holy love, or are we using the care of others to get our own needs met? If we are going to be both effective and healthy as leaders, then it is worth our time to explore what leaves us without healthy boundaries to guide our work.

Codependence Is a Killer

Maybe you've never thought of codependency as something that could apply to you, but let me begin with a typical list of codependent behaviors. This list comes from the Mental Health America website.

The following are just a few of the characteristics of persons challenged with codependent tendencies:

- An exaggerated sense of responsibility for the actions of others
- A tendency to confuse love and pity, along with the tendency to "love" people they can pity and rescue
- A tendency to do more than their share, all the time
- A tendency to become hurt when people don't recognize their efforts
- An unhealthy dependence on relationships. The codependent will do anything to hold on to a relationship to avoid the feeling of abandonment.
- An extreme need for approval and recognition
- A compelling need to control others
- Problems with intimacy/boundaries
- Chronic anger
- Lying/dishonesty
- Difficulty making decisions[16]

With the exception of more obvious and immoral dysfunctions like lying or chronic anger, some of the above issues could be natural (and hopefully occasional) side effects of anyone who cares deeply for a lot of people all the time. But when these traits show up often, in groups, and as a pattern, Houston, we've got a problem.

There are whole books written about the destructive nature of codependence, and you'd do well to dig into this world, not just for your own mental health but for the sake of better training and guiding other leaders in your church.[17] Codependence is a killer. It is often about power and can even be about the need to control others. We may use our need to please others as a way of controlling their response to our presence or controlling their place in our congregation. Under the guise of wanting to love people well, we may be taking too much care of our own need to be needed.[18]

I certainly haven't mastered my own weaknesses in this area. In recent years, I've been dealing with a niggling little health issue that has been hard to treat and very distracting. I've spent more time and money on it than I want to admit, because I can't stand an unanswered question ("Hey, Carolyn—control much?"). Here's the thing: nearly every single article I've read about my issue mentions two things as big culprits—not enough sleep and too much stress. Every time I come across those mentions, I slide by that part of the article *not* because I don't think I have those problems, but because I don't think I can fix them. My life is what it is, to borrow a phrase overused by people who don't want to confront their problems.

As I took my issue to God for healing, I received a huge revelation. I learned something about codependence I don't think I'd ever verbalized in a certain way. What if codependence—which is basically an addiction to people and their interactions with us—leads us to give away more of ourselves than we have to give? What if my body is rebelling against my need to keep everyone happy or my need to stay in control?

I hope you'll stop and reflect for a moment on this symptom of dysfunctional leadership before you move on. If an inward voice is urgently pushing you to skip along to the next topic without looking inward, stop it. What if your body or life or relationships—maybe even your whole congregation—is rebelling because you are giving away more of yourself than you have to give?

Are You the Great Mother?

As I've said already, women in general tend to have a more nurturing, connected approach to relationships. Of course, it can be a glorious gift to be a mother, to have the gift of mothering (whether biologically or spiritually) and to nurture others toward wholeness. It is a joy to communicate the great love of God from a deep well of love and compassion. I celebrate the unique gifts femaleness brings to the work of ministry and believe the body of Christ is better served when women lead. In my surveys of women pastors and church planters, I especially noted and celebrated the ways gender differences enhance our opportunity to serve. When asked, "Do you notice a difference between your leadership style and that of your (male) colleagues?" 88 percent of women said yes. When asked to describe the differences, some women pointed out their more nurturing or "mothering" style of relating to others. One survey respondent wrote, "As the woman, you can give that mother feeling with a listening ear and not worry about what anybody else thinks. That's a DNA you can't change."[19]

She's right. It is DNA we not only *can't* change, we don't *want* to. There are great benefits to connecting in deep and nurturing ways with those who hurt, and women may have the edge in this way. However, even DNA needs to be sanctified. In order to become all God has created us to be, we must acknowledge the tendency to type women leaders as 'ideal mothers' and lead beyond this stereotype.

We still have to contend with our own brokenness and the ways we've overcompensated in some areas to make up for perceived weaknesses in others. We still have to come to terms with how we use or abuse what psychologist Erich Neumann calls the "Great Mother," a phenomenon that may foster leader-centered dependency.[20] A female leader who postures herself as everyone's mom may feel more personal responsibility for the needs of every member. Consider the following comment from a church developer serving in an impoverished area:

> I think we're supposed to be mothers. Mothers. And there is nothing wrong with that, you know? Some of these people need physical love. I have one person that I walked past and touched her shoulder. And probably about three weeks later, she came up to me and she said, "That's the first human touch I've had in two years." And my heart broke. I knew from there on that that's what I'm supposed to do, that this is why God has me in this position. Because I'm supposed to show love.[21]

Where is the line between showing love and becoming the "Great Mother"? When does it become about power or the need to compensate for power we don't think we have? And when does presenting as the "Great Mother" slide right over the line into harboring a savior complex? Devrupa Rakshit of The Swaddle, a web resource that bills itself as "a digital women's health resource," addresses the danger that can accompany work in the helping field:

> Also known as white knight syndrome, savior complex occurs when individuals feel good about themselves only when helping someone, believe their job or purpose is to help those around them, and sacrifice their own interests and well-being in the effort to aid another. Although this knight in shining armor, straight-out-of-a-fairy-tale behavior might sound too good to be true, it's an unhealthy coping mechanism that can do more harm than good . . . While helping people out generally isn't harmful, an individual with savior complex may harm more than they help, by trying to fix something they don't have the skills to fix, rather than entrusting the job to someone who does.[22]

They may find themselves defining their own success by how well they meet the demands of others, much like a mom answering to every need of her child. Harriet Braiker—social and clinical psychologist and author—calls this person the Type E woman.[23] "Type E women want to keep everyone's approval—that is part of how they know that they are succeeding, and they cope with the demands by trying to do it all, often at a substantial cost to their emotional and physical wellbeing."[24] One doesn't have to be a pastor to fall into this trap. Any leader can easily take on more than her fair share of the load.

It can be alluring. When a desperate mom called me, crying and begging for my help with her wayward daughter, I must admit I felt some sense of superiority. The family hadn't attended our church in more than two years (they left to find, as she put it, "a worship service with more fire"). Evidently, they never found what they were looking for and hadn't attended a service anywhere in more than a year. Now there was a family crisis, and they needed a pastor and a community, so she called. I was doing pretty well at holding my boundaries and even asking for some accountability ("Who is providing spiritual support to your family now? What is your plan beyond this call?"). Then the mom said this: "We have been to several churches, *and we even like them better* (yes, she actually said that), but we have never found a pastor like you." I played right into her hands, scheduling an appointment with both mom and daughter at a time that was not convenient for me, so I could "help" a family system I wasn't qualified to help. In a later text, her gratitude convicted me: "Thank you, mama bear." Was this family dramatically transformed by my "help"? Nope. Nothing changed.

Taking Comfort from Misinterpreted Care

Helping, even when helping hurts, is often what we'll do first because it *feels* right. Gail Dudley, author, advocate, ordained pastor, and publisher of Ready Publications, writes,

> As a pastor and because I love people and ministry, I thought I needed to be completely open and vulnerable

to everyone. Other mature Christians tried to help me understand how to be honest, but not overly vulnerable. Thinking I knew better, I did not heed their advice. Big mistake. I quickly learned how some individuals within the congregation took advantage of me, appearing to be interested in a friendship, but only wanting to be my friend for their gain. After several years of this, I found myself somewhat isolated because I built walls to protect myself. Now, I have been gradually working my way back to the middle, but this time with more wisdom and godly maturity.[25]

When our desire to be vulnerable in our care for souls is abused, we get burned. The ground becomes even more shaky when pastoral care is misinterpreted. Women may find the nurturing work of pastoral care to be so natural that they don't even think about how it may be received. I remember a time when a man in our community got angry with me. I had not given in to his preferences in some leadership decision or another, and he was clearly interested in having more power and voice in our church than he was being given. When things didn't go his way, he called a meeting of several leaders and planned to school us in "empowerment of the laity." The day came for the meeting, and my disgruntled parishioner walked in with a stack of our denominational rule books in his hand. When he set them in the middle of the table, it was clear he planned to school us in what it means to be in our "tribe." Before he could start, another man in the room looked at the stack of books, reached for his own Bible, and laid it on top of the stack. It was a brilliant move. The angry guy was left with no power in the conversation. And while I was grateful for the moment and the "win," I was also left feeling a lot of compassion toward the losing soul. After the meeting, I hugged him like a mom would hug a hurting child. It was the wrong thing to do. That gesture was sorely misinterpreted and fed our continued inability to communicate in healthy ways. The crazy thing is that I didn't immediately learn from it, mostly because I didn't immediately know my gesture had been misinterpreted. It would be years before I'd come to understand the power of a hug and the need to use that gesture wisely in the work of leadership.

In an article titled "When Men Misinterpret Pastoral Care," Katherine Pershey, pastor and author, writes about the issues inherent in women's leadership as they pertain to boundaries. "The best-case scenario for women is that they will minister in congregations that cultivate healthy boundaries and strong lay leadership . . . [yet] in many church cultures, women in ministry are a recent reality. It is still new and novel for men to receive spiritual guidance from a female pastor."[26] Pershey quotes women spiritual leaders who notice how men receive them—some with heightened interest, others vying for power. The best antidote seems to be a solid system that makes use of a team of laypersons with a flattened power structure, so that everyone serves and is served with care.

What Is Love?

Consider this verse from 2 John 1: "Watch out that you do not lose what we have worked for, but that you may be rewarded fully" (v. 8). That's a good line. It reminds me that I can damage my own progress or the progress of my church by giving in to cheap versions of love that have nothing to do with Jesus or the kingdom of God.

John's second pastoral letter is written to "a lady." Some say it was an actual woman, others say that "lady" is code for "church." Either way, it works for us. This is a word for women who lead and for the church about truth and love.

Verse 6 is the key. John writes, "This is love: that we walk in obedience to his commands. As you have heard from the beginning, his command is that you walk in love." No other writer in the whole Bible uses the word *love* as much as John (57 times in the gospel of John—more often than all the other gospels combined—and 44 times in 1 John). John was completely taken by Jesus's command to love. He was infected by the love of Jesus, and he understood that biblical love is defined by obedience to God's commands, not by how nice we are to people (although that will be a side effect). And John comes back to this refrain over and over:

- If anyone obeys [God's] word, love for God is truly made complete in them (1 John 2:5).
- We know that we have come to know him if we keep his commands (1 John 2:3).
- Anyone who does not do what is right is not God's child, nor is anyone who does not love their brother or sister (1 John 3:10).
- Dear children, let us not love with words or speech but with actions and in truth (1 John 3:18).
- This is how we know that we love the children of God: by loving God and carrying out his commands (1 John 5:2).
- In fact, this is love for God: to keep his commands (1 John 5:3).

For John, there is no doubt that love for God is authenticated and proven by obedience to his commands. "And now, dear lady, I am not writing you a new command but one we have had from the beginning. I ask that we love one another. And this is love: that we walk in obedience to his commands" (2 John 5–6).

Somehow, this message is for us, too, as we struggle past our all-too-human tendencies to "fix" or to "please" or to work overtime to get the approval of others. It is our word as we default to lesser gifts, when God has called us to greater works. It is our word as we give away more of ourselves than we have to give. This is what I mean when I say "cheap love." To walk in love is to walk in obedience to God, to remember that he is God, and we are not. It is to trust our people and our reputation to his care so we can do the work he has given us.

Perhaps God wants to do much more through you and me than help people feel better. The more we work to define ourselves by how God sees us, the more we will have healthy responses in the moment-by-moment pastoral care opportunities.

CHAPTER 5

THE BIOLOGICAL BARRIER

*The Very Real Thing Nobody
Likes to Talk About*

"I'm afraid you love your work more than you love me."

This was the line that woke me up while I was falling in love with a vision for a new church. I'd been consumed for years with the idea of starting something new, so by the time I was given a chance, I was full of vision and energy. I knew exactly what to do, who to call, what to order, how to organize. I was remarkably busy and happy—right up through the end of the first month. I came up for air just in time to hear my husband say, "I am afraid you love your work more than you love me."

I couldn't imagine him thinking that. I love my husband deeply. We've been partners in our work from day one. He could sense God's call on my life even on our first date, while I held a cigarette in one hand and a beer in the other (the man has an amazing ability to see beyond the obvious). I stepped into my call to spiritual leadership on the strength of his encouragement, but by the time we were planting a church, I was in up to my neck. Or maybe over my head.

I'm afraid you love your work more than you love me.

To alleviate Steve's fear, I stopped talking so much about the church at home, thinking that would help. I really did try to keep "work" at work, but it was almost as if I was trying to plant a church without anyone noticing. I'd wait until my family got out the door in the morning, then I'd set about doing everything I'd already been doing and then some. I wore myself out. I wore my family out. But I didn't know how to stop.

If I'd known then what I know now, I might have navigated things differently. I know now that women *can* have it all, but not necessarily all *at once*. I know now that if it is God's work, God will see it through. I also know now that counting the cost is a critical factor in navigating the demands of leadership. I needed seasoned voices in my life to help me understand what happens emotionally, spiritually, and even physically when women lead.

Spiritual leadership can be exhausting. For women, the strain can be severe, and not just for the reasons we've already mentioned. From the childbearing years to midlife, women experience distinctive seasons that affect *everything*. We bear children, bear the responsibility of mothering, and bear up under the challenges of midlife, all while learning to lead and live well both in ministry and life. All of it carries a certain tension.

Maternity and Ministry: A Holy Tension

Early in adulthood, any women gifted for leadership will find themselves with significant choices to make about life and family, call and career. They'll make choices about when or if to marry, when or if to have children.[1] Will they have children first, then pursue the call to ministry? Pursue the call first? Or attempt both simultaneously? And how will children fit into an irregular schedule, especially if the spouse is equally engaged in his work? These are huge questions, and while there are no "right" or "wrong" answers, a woman will certainly need to count the cost of her decisions and take nothing for granted because, for women who lead, the pendulum swings easily from feeling overly guilty to feeling overly tired. How do we do it all? *Can* we do it all?

It is important to set this conversation in a historical context. For thousands of years, the primary economic unit in agrarian societies was the family. On farms, everybody—husbands, wives, and children—produced and contributed. Then, in the nineteenth century, the growing affluence resulting from the Industrial Revolution in Britain and America made it possible for a single income to support a family. The expectation spread that women should devote themselves to the "private sphere" of the home. By the twentieth century, this idea had been embraced by white, Protestant, middle- and upper-class families in cities. Thus, the "stay-at-home mom" as suburban norm was born. Historians call it the "cult of domesticity." It waxed and waned depending on economic conditions but did not extend to farming families or to working-class immigrants and minorities, who needed two incomes and who often worked for middle- and upper-class families as domestic servants.

The generation of professional women who first walked boldly back into the workforce discovered that taking on a full-time job didn't necessarily mean they'd have someone sharing the load at home. In a column about the women's liberation movement of the 1960s and '70s, Lisa Davis writes,

> For many entering the work force for the first time, working didn't turn out to be liberation as much as a second set of responsibilities added to women's already full plates, as many feminists, economists and journalists have noted . . . That existence was so taxing that in 1984 the writer Marjorie Hansen Shaevitz coined the term Superwoman Syndrome. "I found that, professionally, some women were at the top of their field," Ms. Shaevitz said. But "emotionally and personally, they were a mess" . . . Some studies have found the do-it-all expectation is particularly trying for Black women and contributes to health disparities.[2]

As Dr. Cheryl Bridges Johns, pastor and seminary professor, said of women coming of age in the '60s and '70s, "We had to find our identity pretty early, and then had to rush toward it."[3] This wasn't necessarily a good thing. Many women found themselves burned out by vocations that should have enriched their lives. The grace embedded in the experience of our mothers and grandmothers is the lesson that "can" doesn't necessarily mean "should."

Yet here we are, in an era when women have every option available. The expectations placed on young, gifted women can be brutal. One leader I interviewed had a particularly compelling story. Recently graduated from seminary, she and her husband had planned to move back to their home state to serve a local church. They expected to share a post and a pace they could sustain while they began their own family. Almost immediately, she was tapped by denominational leaders to plant a church. She attempted to decline but was told that wasn't an option. "They sent me to [church-planting] boot camp, and I showed up with my son, who was still nursing, and my mom, who was going to watch him while I was in session. [The training consultant] said, 'Moms don't plant.' I didn't want to do it, and no one thought I could do it. The coach they assigned to me thought it was a joke."[4]

Yet there she was, a brand-new mother, recent seminary graduate, and church planter stuck in a complicated situation. Rather than derailing her career, she gave herself to the work with the best attitude possible. Meanwhile, she and her husband continued to work toward their family goals. "I found out I was pregnant again the day before our launch. That timing—birthing a daughter and a church in the same year—that's probably the hardest year of my ministry."[5] Finding support for her situation was difficult:

> I thought women would be [those] I could go to for encouragement and support but that has not been the case . . . The pastor of the anchor church was a woman . . . she let me know if I did things my way instead of her way, things would not go well with me . . . When I shared with her that I was pregnant with my daughter, she said, "I thought you were more committed to the church." She said it was irresponsible of me to have more than one child when God needed so much. That was hard to hear. She said, "Your kids are a liability now in my ministry in the church."[6]

Harsh, right? But not uncommon. *Harvard Business Review* reports studies of employees who became parents. Women found their careers derailed; if they chose to have children while pursuing career goals, they often sacrificed power, status, and income.[7] As it turns out, biology has cultural implications, both in the workplace and at home. There is an expectation, usually unspoken, that working women will still carry more of the load at home than their husbands in the form of housekeeping and parenting.[8] In her TED talk about women in leadership, Sheryl Sandberg makes the same claim: "The data shows . . . if a woman and a man work full-time and have a child, the woman does twice the amount of housework the man does, and the woman does three times the amount of childcare than the man does."[9] Given that there are only twenty-four hours in anyone's day, that means less time available for work (which is not the same as having less work to do) and, often, more stress.

None of this is to say that it's all fun and games for men who pursue a family while growing a ministry career. Having heard the laments of my male colleagues, I'm aware that our struggles have more in common than in contrast. Men face their own challenges on the way to effective leadership. What we *can* say is that being female means a kind of double bind when it comes to work and family. If we have children, we'll work harder both at home *and* at work. Women leaders in and beyond ministry can attest to the differences between how men and women process the good work of parenting. "There's just a difference between the way a mother and a father look at their kids and the sense of responsibility that they feel," said a woman interviewed for the *Harvard Business Review* article. "I feel my male counterparts can more easily disconnect from what's happening at home . . . If I did sort of disconnect, things wouldn't fall apart, but I wouldn't feel good about it, so it's just not going to happen."[10] Women are more likely to take responsibility for meal prep and grocery shopping, birthday parties and home decor. All those tasks add up to roughly a double shift every working day for most women. For women, having children often means putting career advancement at risk.

Then there's the guilt. Though "mom guilt" as a phenomenon first appeared in the latter decades of the twentieth century, it is deeply embedded in the psyche of contemporary women. We are beating ourselves up over a blip on the world's timeline. Nonetheless, the struggle is real. Women are quick to suspect they've overlooked something important (whatever that "something" is), that if their children suffer in any way, it's their fault.[11] Women leaders may be killing it on the home front—attending all the soccer games, packing all the lunches, hanging out at bedtime—but can still not only feel inadequate but be perceived and critiqued as shortchanging the family. As Dr. Bridges Johns said of expectations one generation has laid on the next, "The very things we'd tell them to do in order to empower them has become a sentence spoken over their lives."[12]

We women leaders may have mastered the art of multitasking and balancing, even camouflaging our stress and our worn-out spirits so that our careers and families can survive. But too often, we do this to the detriment of our mental and physical health, our important relationships, and our own spirituality. Balancing motherhood, vocation, and home life is a stretch for anyone and difficult to sustain for any length of time. In my conversations with female spiritual leaders, many discussed the very real challenge of juggling the mother/wife/pastor role:

This is something I feel I hear from every female pastor that I never hear from any male pastor: How am I balancing family life and pastoring? My kids are still very little. How am I able to be present to them fully without neglecting, and how am I able to be present to work, you know?

It's the *hardest* thing to balance ever. [I'm] grateful for kids who get it but always feel like I'm choosing, and that's hard.

The demand on time has been very challenging. I have become a much more empathetic and compassionate pastor in regard to other parents/young families.

My kids still need—and I'm not talking about some youth that you put in the back room—actual childcare that I can trust my child to, not just who you can rustle up. How are we going to afford that?

I often felt guilty for the hours I worked and the blurring of my work and private life.[13]

It doesn't end with how we process our own circumstances. That same *Harvard Business Review* article I quoted earlier noted the difference in the way others process women leaders with kids. In interviews with very successful women (for instance, partners in law firms), "we heard them routinely described as bad mothers—'horrible' women who were not 'positive role models of working moms.'"[14] Yet, the system continues to use women for its own ends. In their desire to increase female representation on boards and in leadership positions, the powers-that-be tug on the time and energy of the smaller pool of women who are available. Women may be asked to speak, lead, and serve at a greater rate simply because there are so few of them in spiritual leadership. Many women, wanting to both advocate and take advantage of such offers, will say yes, only to find themselves stretched by too many commitments. All the while, they drag behind them a wagonload of guilt for all they feel they are missing at home. Blessed are the trailblazers if they love their work, for they assuredly have more work to love.

What If I Just Stay Single?

I love Paul. No one beyond Jesus has had more impact on how we think as Christians and particularly as Christian leaders. Paul has also had a tremendous impact on how we understand the spiritual leadership of women, though I'm convinced he is sadly misunderstood on this point (see Romans 16). He emphasized the work of an elder (Titus 1) and helped us define not only marriage and gender, but also the sacrifice required for spiritual leadership. As a single man (by choice, as best we can tell), Paul was in a unique position to talk about what it means to remain single for the cause of Christ. He provided that example for those called to the kind of kingdom work that requires a single-minded focus.

Singleness is a more acceptable option today than it has ever been, at least in the Western world. A Pew Research survey has shown that in the last several decades, "marriage rates have declined, particularly among younger Americans.

Today, 18 percent of adults younger than 30 are married, compared with 31 percent in 1995."[15] For women pursuing ministry leadership, this growing trend presents more options. On one hand, singleness may make one more "portable." On the other hand, it may leave a leader in a vulnerable and isolated place as she takes responsibility for the spiritual lives of others.[16] For some women, singleness will be a calling; for others, it will be a fact of life. Choosing singleness may mean grieving children she won't have or making space for children in a single-parent home. For those who receive singleness as part of the greater call, community becomes essential. But if the ministry system a woman is in requires or promotes itinerancy, the system may work against her emotional or relational health.

In my conversations with women leaders, more than half reported working fifty or more hours per week. And they felt it. They said things like, "I need a nap!" and, "I feel as though it's a young person's game." Older women realized they didn't have the energy for growing ministries. Several admitted they were just going through the motions and felt burned out. Some were on antidepressants; a quarter of those I talked to were seeing a therapist. One said simply, "I drink more."[17]

You'd think the antidote would be to simply give women a break. Offer them fewer hours on the job or a more flexible schedule. Wouldn't that help? Well, yes and no. Go back to that *Harvard Business Review* article which reported on interviews with employees at high-end firms. Women in those firms reported feeling personally conflicted about the long hours and daily schedule fluctuations requiring them to constantly choose between work and family. When they complained, the firm's leaders listened and gave them more opportunities for creating flexible schedules and working fewer hours. Problem solved, right?

Not exactly. Women who made those choices found themselves effectively excluded from advancement toward upper-level positions and eventual partnerships.[18] No one planned for that consequence, nor is there an easy way around it. Every road seems to lead to another double bind. The real demon, these authors conclude, is something deeper than gender. It is the general culture of overwork, a culture that hurts both men and women. Surely this is not God's best for anyone.

Can I Love My Work If I'm a Mom?

It's a hard fact that, in the middle of life, leaders will wrestle with their relationships to both their work and children. It isn't just about juggling soccer practice or driving lessons. It is also about the feelings children have about their mom's vocation. In her book, *Doing Leadership Differently*, author and professor Amanda Sinclair talks about the interesting dynamic often in play between successful mothers and their daughters. Women want to be positive role models for their daughters, but there is an edge to it. "If they've been successful or had a public profile, there can be resentment about mothers putting themselves first." Sinclair detected a pattern among these daughters: "Women leaders tend to exhibit a pattern of parental influence where fathers are regarded affectionately, even adored, while mothers, particularly those who have achieved, are regarded more ambivalently."[19]

Let's go ahead and state the obvious. Having a mom who is a pastor is peculiar, as Cheryl Bridges Johns notes:

The oddity is the mother who is in Christian leadership. That's just odd. Daughters grow up with an oddity for a mother, which may contribute to this ambivalence. As much as we try to say, "We're not putting pressure on you," [a daughter] will feel that pressure to be what we are. Or they will deal with the weirdness of us as part of their own story. "Yes, my mother is a pastor, even if you don't believe in her. And maybe, even if I don't believe in her."[20]

Hearing Johns voice it just this way was revelatory for me. I hadn't fully considered all the subtle ways my vocation has been part of my daughter's story—that it might not have been the five-star experience for her that it has been for me (well, maybe not quite five stars for me, either). Yet somehow, she has been able to absorb and process the experience positively. In our conversations, she can say her childhood experience of church, Jesus, and family life was life-giving.

Mandy Smith (another wonderful Australian who is a pastor and author) had a similar conversation with her daughter, which they shared in an article for *Christianity Today*. She writes,

There have been many days in the past 10 years since I became pastor when I have been so overwhelmed, trying to be my own role model (as my friend Tara Beth Leach calls it) that I didn't have a lot of time to wonder how my daughter was taking it all in. But now, as I watch her flourishing, stepping with confidence into her gifts, being resilient and faithful, I am overwhelmed with gratitude that somehow God has brought us both through my fumblings and fears.[21]

Other moms in leadership roles have found ways to spin their circumstances positively. "My role as a parent . . . did make me a better pastor. It made me more compassionate and helped me to better understand the feelings and motivations of others. It also gave me confidence in taking authority." Others said:

I was able to work my schedule around my children's activities . . . [My kids] have helped me develop patience and have helped me connect to others in the community.

I set clear boundaries and made purposeful time for family, only allowing true emergencies to infringe on that family time and space. I appreciate the flexibility of a pastor's schedule in the role of parenting.

It has strengthened me spiritually and given me a stronger sense of connection with other parents.[22]

I can certainly resonate with the positives. I know it doesn't always turn out well, but I will forever be grateful for the grace that saw my child into a faithful and productive adulthood and into choices that allow her to fully live out her gifts and contribute beautifully to the world.

And Then There's Menopause

As if finding the right time for pregnancy, birth, and raising children weren't enough, women also face midlife issues that can complicate the work-life balance (actually, I think balance is a myth, but I'll say more about that later).

Menopause can be emotional, draining, confusing. "The constant change of hormone levels during this time," writes medical journalist Colette Bouchez, "can have a troubling effect on emotions . . . leaving some women to feel irritable and even depressed."[23] Navigating this season of life well while carrying on the work of church leadership and development requires sensitivity and realism.

I have quoted Cheryl Bridges Johns liberally in this chapter because I've been personally inspired and helped by her wisdom, particularly when it comes to the life stages of women leaders. She has written extensively on the gifts of these biological markers in midlife, especially. "As we enter menopause," she writes, "much of the unfinished business of our earlier lives returns to haunt us. Standing at the threshold of the second half of life, we bring all this baggage with us. It is time to make peace with our past and with one another."[24] Johns compares the turbulence of puberty with the turbulence of the menopausal years, and she warns women to avoid masking emotions during the journey. Culture wants women to somehow maintain youthful markers and minimize emotional shifts and revelations. Johns gets particularly honest about the anger that often surfaces in these years and writes about the accumulating emotional debt accrued as women age—a debt that comes due in midlife. "The problem that needs to be addressed is not our hormone levels. It is our anger levels."[25] Feelings, memories, and relational regrets become more intense. There is literally a chemical reaction taking place in our brains that releases stored or repressed memories. All these chemical, emotional, and physical changes are getting us ready for the rest of our lives. Yet, for all its "normalcy," menopausal women are rarely informed, often medicated, and encouraged to stifle the wide range of emotions that surface as they shift into a new phase of life. As Johns warns, "Remember this: when not allowed to express anger, the body turns on itself . . . Sadly, it is more acceptable for women to be ill than angry."[26]

This season is not for wimps, but I probably don't have to tell you that. What often goes unnoticed, however, is the gift embedded in the journey through midlife and menopause. Rather than pushing through, as we might have done when we were young, we discover we don't have to push through. If we can withstand the cultural pressure, we can find a more authentic way to be present to ourselves and the world. In my conversations with women who lead in midlife, this shift in thinking was palpable and had positive effects:

I have several chronic illnesses, and as I age, I have to be more aware of my body and its messages for rest and renewal.

The only change in my health is that I now have to do breathing techniques to lower my heart rate under stress.

I don't have the stamina I had ten years ago. On the other hand, it has made me more compassionate for the elderly and their contributions.

I work out, ride my bike, and play tennis. Being fit physically, spiritually, and mentally is important. As one experiences life, one understands the depth of the Bible more.

(Midlife) has finally forced me to learn how to delegate.

[It] makes me think more and plan better just to use my time and energy where I'm needed and useful.[27]

Midlife is an opportunity for both men and women to move into new spiritual rooms and explore new ways of living more deeply into the Spirit. Doing so while on public display as a spiritual leader requires a lot of self-reflection, prayer, support, and intentional time apart. Women need permission to do the work of leading but with time for rest, Sabbath, and family. Training should have the needs of women in mind, since the rhythms of a woman's life are different than those of men, many of whom are able to work while their wives stay at home (we'll talk more in part 2 about all the training we ought to seek out). For women, healthy rhythms are not solved by simply advising more time off. The challenge may not be solvable at all without the guidance of God. Every female leader—indeed, every *leader*—probably needs to place a sticky note on the bathroom mirror that says, "It isn't all up to you." Because friends, this—and by "this," I mean leadership, calling, life, stages, *all of this*—is very much a work of the Spirit.

Think Rhythm, Not Balance

I have a secret for you: balance is a myth. We know it because the quest for balance tends to be guilt-producing. Balance tries to get me to believe that I can carve my life up into equal parts that all have their own little categories, but that isn't how life works. It isn't how we are designed. In fact, this is part of what makes our society so dysfunctional. When we compartmentalize—church goes in this slot, work goes in this slot, family over here, God over here—we train our minds to separate rather than integrate. This is not to say that we won't get overextended or that our priorities won't get out of whack. I'm just saying that a lot of the rhetoric out there creates the illusion that we can divide our lives into equal pieces and somehow make it all fit. This isn't the principle behind Sabbath. Sabbath says that God is Lord over all of it, and that rather than striking *balance* between the pieces of us, the call is to a holy *rhythm* of work and rest.

Somewhere along the way, a friend in ministry who was walking through a valley emailed me a profound question. Here's how she framed it:

> I've wrestled a lot because, in years of child-raising and empty bank accounts and job loss and disrespect or whatever particular tornado was ripping through life, sometimes the most I could do was brush my teeth, take a shower, hold a toddler, read the devotional email in my inbox—or not—plead [in my] prayers, and nap.
>
> So here's my real question: What do spiritual disciplines look like during seasons of life when you barely have the emotional energy to take a shower? What's manageable or kind or reasonable for people who are stumbling out of a dark place?[28]

It's a great question, isn't it? What do spiritual disciplines look like during seasons of life when you barely have the emotional energy to take a shower? I reminded her that disciplines are not for people who have too much time on their hands. Disciplines are for people who have too many *distractions*. In my own pursuit of a holy rhythm, I've discovered a truth: discipline is rest. Remember that rest as the Bible defines it is not a cure for exhaustion but a pathway to assurance. That's what boundaries are at their roots. They are a discipline that promotes rest and rejects guilt. Discipline creates rhythm, which creates space, which creates rest, which leads to joy.

Spiritual disciplines are both rooted in and lead back to Sabbath. Sabbath is the anchor to a life of holy rhythm. I love how Jesus's merciful invitation into a holy rhythm is worded in *The Message* version of Matthew 11:28–30:

> Are you tired? Worn out? Burned out on religion? Come to me. Get away with me and you'll recover your life. I'll show you how to take a real rest. Walk with me and work with me—watch how I do it. Learn the unforced rhythms of grace. I won't lay anything heavy or ill-fitting on you. Keep company with me and you'll learn to live freely and lightly.

I want that life. I want to learn the unforced rhythms of grace. Jesus tells me I have continual access to these unforced rhythms as I surrender my will to his. But lest we sound too optimistic (not to mention too "Christianese"), we must acknowledge that spiritual disciplines can also be frustrating, elusive, sometimes impossible. The demands of spiritual leadership can be bone-crushing at times (even for the Son of God). God's grace and power are real. So is the battle.

Having acknowledged that reality, Amanda Sinclair tells us, "leadership is an idea available for us to shape and re-form."[29] From childbearing, to intentional singleness, from midlife, to the elder role, the seasons of our lives allow multiple windows of opportunity for us to shape and re-form our voice and style, rhythm and gifts. When we receive this as a grace, we begin to see the world—and our world—more creatively. Perhaps when we do, we will become willing to let the Holy Spirit show us the unforced rhythms of grace already embedded in our circumstances, which allow us to live out our created design in ways that bless the world, bless us, and bless those we love most.

PART 2

EMPOWERING WOMEN TO LEAD AND SUCCEED

Now that we have acknowledged that women come into leadership facing multiple challenges, it is time to ask a practical question:

> What will help women navigate those barriers so they
> can lead successfully from a whole and holy place?

What we've learned so far is that solid preparation and the right tools can mean the difference between success and failure for a spiritual leader. We also know that by leaning in and caring actively for women in spiritual leadership, we care well for a theology that makes room for women at the table. We collectively determine that we will not be so pragmatic in our pursuit of church development (in other words, not so enamored of traditional methods of church growth) that we leave women behind, effectively cutting ourselves off at the knees. Men and women called by God into spiritual leadership are invited into nothing less than the answer to Jesus's own prayer: "Your kingdom come, your will be done, on earth as it is in heaven" (Matt. 6:10). Leaders who are deeply passionate about the fulfillment of this prayer ought to aspire to kingdom greatness and ought to have every resource at their disposal to do the work well.

As Jim Collins, author of *Good to Great*, has written, when what you are good at comes together with what you are passionate about, "not only does your work move toward greatness, but so does your life."[1] That's the point of the remainder of this book: to help women and those who advocate for their place as leaders think seriously about how to be great at what we are called to do. Because friends, let's face it: the church of Jesus Christ has met its quota of spiritual leaders who are underprepared and underqualified for the challenging work of kingdom-building. The church is starving for leaders who are called, passionate, and prepared, so let's talk about how to make that happen. We turn our attention first to the issue of identity: knowing who you are in Christ.

CHAPTER 6

IDENTITY

Knowing Who You Are Is (Almost) Everything

When you're miserable or broke or desperate, you can talk yourself into believing just about anything. But the night I said yes to the call to ministry, I wasn't any of those things. I was happily married with a home, a child, and a good job. In the midst of my middle-class stability, I was simply wondering aloud in the presence of the Holy Spirit if a child, a house, two cars, and two stable jobs was all there was to life. God responded, "Just say yes." It was as clear a supernatural word as the first time I'd heard his voice at the age of thirteen, when he invited me to take up a call to preach and lead. Back then, I lacked the emotional and relational resources to follow that call. This time around, with the support of my husband and the hard-won wisdom of life experience, I was able to more confidently say yes. I have been pursuing this call since 1995.

My daughter was four years old when we moved to

Kentucky to attend seminary, so for virtually all her life, a pastor-mom is all she has known. This makes her perspective very different from mine. (She once asked me from the back seat of the car, "Mama, can boys be preachers, too?") Her perspective is not the norm, even among others her age. I recently chatted with a dozen middle and high school students about life and ministry. These kids were everything from believers to skeptics. Several had never gone to any church but ours, meaning they'd never known anything but a female pastor. Toward the end of our conversation, one student asked, "Does anyone ever question your role as a pastor?" I had to laugh.

She seemed almost relieved, like she'd been worried that no one had mentioned it to me. This was a young woman who'd had no church in her life before ours. She had come to Christ just a year or so prior, so she had no theology to wrap around her question, just the experience of neighbors, friends, and family members who questioned her attendance at the church where she'd heard the gospel and accepted Christ's redemption—the same church where the pastor is a woman.

During that conversation, several other students echoed my young friend's thoughts. I was surprised, even though I know it isn't a cultural issue but one of human fallenness (and last time I checked, we're still fallen). The present generation is dealing with so many gender and identity issues that you'd think my role as a leader would be the least of their concerns. Through that conversation, I was made freshly aware that not only these kids but most of the people in my church fight an internal battle just to be there, because the person who leads them spiritually is female. I'm humbled by the thought that for many in my congregation, it would be easier to leave than to stay and defend our set of circumstances as biblical. After all, this is not likely their hill to die on.

Not every woman reading this book will be a lead or solo pastor at a church, but the truth is that every woman, regardless of her role, will face challenges to her spiritual leadership at times. In chapter 2, we talked about perception as a barrier—both others' perceptions and our own—and acknowledged a fallen human tendency toward hierarchies. Since Genesis 3, we've all been conditioned to mentally assess who is "greater than" and who is "less than." Across the world, women overwhelmingly end up on the "less than" end of that equation. This is a fallen view of the world and one from which we are all trying to recover. Learning who we are in Christ is a big part of healing from our fallenness. Women need strategies to develop their own voice, authority, and sense of identity as leaders. So let's talk more about perception and identity.

In my research on women who lead, I discovered that in addition to women who might feel uncertain about their competencies, there are others whose sense of "self" or calling deeply impacted their confidence as ministry leaders. Ten percent of those interviewed indicated faith in the idea that their lives have purpose, yet they struggled to understand what that purpose is. Another 6 percent reported that they were just going through the motions and felt burned out. One person went so far as to say she was struggling with being able to define who she was, *period*. The ministry had completely unhinged her from her sense of self and, clearly, it was affecting her ministry. In my (admittedly limited) sampling, roughly one in five women wrestled with issues related to identity.[1]

Not knowing who one is, especially as it relates to faith in Christ as the author of one's identity, can be devastating. Nothing can derail a call to ministry more quickly. One woman said, "I am my biggest challenge; I need to get out of my own way. I have no doubt I'm called to be where I'm at, doing what I'm doing, yet I often think could I be more effective doing something else. I don't know what that would look like. Is that me just trying to get out of this?" Another woman noted the added pressure of her minority status: "Knowing that I am a minority [in both race and gender] among pastors, there is an underlying pressure that my success matters." Yet another beleaguered spiritual leader wrote, "Folks are expecting me to fail either at ministry or motherhood."[2] That pressure to excel in multiple directions, and to do so publicly, creates a real identity crisis. Who are we primarily? Who are we *really*? How does the call to ministry factor into our answer to those questions?

I remember being on the phone with a woman who had been deeply wounded by the unraveling of her reputation after resigning from the church she served. Things had been fine; in fact, she left on good terms in order to move closer to family. But after she left, other staffers felt free to critique her leadership. When comments found their way back to her, the effect was demoralizing. She later wrote me to reflect on what the experience was teaching her:

> As I pray, I'm sensing that one dynamic is the way that men and younger people in general expect older women [she was in her early fifties] to bear the emotional and spiritual burden of things. I've thrown myself under the bus many times for them, so I suppose it's easy for them

to think that's the best way to fix this problem, too. What's done is done, and I'm finding peace with the fact that they will not understand the situation as I do. I am trying to understand the dynamic for the sake of my own peace in future roles and for the sake of other women.

Just as it might seem easier for a parishioner to leave a female-pastored church than to stay, it is also easier for the pastor herself to leave than to stay. As a denominational consultant with whom I spoke noted, "Our women pastors and pastors of color don't tend to grow larger churches because they don't tend to stay at them. This is an issue with all our women leaders and our leaders of color. They tend to get sucked into the administrative structure of the denomination."[3] The United Methodist Clergywomen Retention Study, conducted by the Anna Howard Shaw Center at Boston University (a center for women in ministry) confirms this pattern.[4] This study has been tracking women in leadership for thirty-five years. At the heart of it is the question, "Why do so many women leave ministry after five years of starting ministry?" They've tracked the pattern. Something like three-quarters of women leave after five years, and women leave ministry at a higher rate than men. The trend my colleague noticed of women being drawn into administrative roles and away from parish ministry (when parish ministry might have been their first love) is one of the more notable statistics coming out of this research.

For this reason alone, investing time in understanding who we are in Christ and how that identity is lived out daily in work and interactions becomes critical. Authenticity is important to the role of spiritual leadership. It is expected, but it only works if you have confidence in your sense of calling and have taken authority over your role. People seeking a deeper relationship with Jesus do not need a performer. They also don't need an emotional basket case. What most folks want from a leader, whether they know how to articulate it or not, is a display of authentic strength they can count on, that allows them a little room to be weak without feeling they'll bring someone's whole ministry crashing down. This means that those of us who lead must do the spiritual and emotional work to know who we are and what we've been called to do in this world.

So how can we help women find courage to stand firm in the midst of challenging seasons without fear of how they'll be perceived by others? I believe it begins with identity—knowing who you are in Christ.

Have You Learned You?

I want to ask you to do an exercise. You'll need a pen and something to write on. At the top of a blank page, write the words: "I am . . ." Remember that this is the name by which God revealed himself to Moses (Ex. 3:14). It is also a complete sentence. But here, in this exercise, these are the first two words of a sentence you're being asked to complete. Let yourself listen for a moment to your inner voice as it stretches to finish that sentence.

"I am . . ."

I've done this exercise with roomfuls of people and often notice that completing this one statement can reduce people to tears. Why? Often, we have not allowed ourselves to acknowledge what we believe about ourselves deep down. If the sentence you've just created brings on a moment of raw vulnerability, confession, or even numbness, take a moment to sit with that feeling in the presence of God.

Now, here's what I want you to do next. Once you've finished that first sentence, I want you to continue writing "I am" statements. You may find as you begin that the first statements to surface are more relational. "I am a mom." "I am a sister." "I am a leader." If you continue to write, you should eventually begin to find words that describe your essence. "I am creative." "I am joyful." Or even, "I am depressed." You may start a sentence with "I am one who . . ." as in "I am one who cares about my health," or "I am one who gets angry in traffic." The one rule in this exercise is that every sentence must begin with "I am" (Note: "*I am not* . . ." statements are off-limits; this is not about who you are *not*, but about who you *are)*.

I learned this exercise from a counselor who often invites his clients to write two thousand "I am" statements as part of basic identity work.[5] Yes, you read correctly: two *thousand*. I never made it that far with my list, but after writing nearly a thousand statements, I began to understand the value of not stopping after fifty or a hundred. It tends to take us a while to get honest with ourselves. When we first start writing, our statements sound more like a personal public relations campaign. We emphasize the positives. But somewhere around four or five hundred, we begin to get very honest with God and ourselves.

Some of my "I am" statements later on in the process brought to the surface things I might never have consciously acknowledged otherwise. When I wrote, "I am one with nervous hands," that totally opened up a whole conversation with God about my issue with low-grade, chronic anxiety.

I also wrote things like:

I am embarrassed by failure.
I am competitive.
I am envious of others' success.

On a particularly difficult day, I wrote, "I am suspicious of God." That sent me digging all around the roots of my own trust issues and what I really believe about what God is doing in and through my life. That was hard but good work. I no longer believe that statement is true of me. I ultimately discovered that it's *me* I don't trust, not God. Learning (or admitting) that about myself may not result in deep healing, but at least it is progress.

One day, as I continued to write "I am" statements, it finally dawned on me what the whole project was about: "I am trying to learn Carolyn." In the middle of my life and deep into my vocation, I was finally figuring out who I am in relation to God, myself, and the people I serve. This is the work we are all challenged to do, especially as we put ourselves out there in leadership and service. We all want to be the most authentic and confident versions of ourselves before God and others. Women who struggle with a negative self-image or no sense of their identity in Christ will find themselves on a steeper climb than those who don't. Sometimes a negative self-image can manifest itself as self-protectiveness or lower self-esteem. It is what I like to call the "protective crouch." A person with a weakened sense of identity will create a defense that puts others in an uncomfortable place. A negative thought process tends to make women—to make *anyone*—more prone to a defensive posture, less assertive, less confident, and less attractive as a leader.

Meanwhile, when we see ourselves as worthy—not by

our own merit, but through Christ—others benefit from our confidence. We are presenting ourselves to the world in a form that most closely aligns with our pre-Genesis 3 design. Who am I *really*? Who am I *in Christ*? To make room for who we are—the artist, the lover, the friend, the athlete, the fill-in-the-blank—we have to value time with the One who designed us, who called us into being, who called us good. We discover very quickly that there are far too many voices out there that want to speak into our lives and shape our choices, and many of them do not call us "good."

So how do we deal with the issue of our own identity? What does it mean to know who I am in Christ? And why does it matter so much, especially on the tough days?

Neil Anderson, in his classic work, *Who I Am in Christ*, calls this the most important task:

> The most important belief that we possess is a true knowledge of who God is. The second most important belief is who we are as children of God, because we cannot consistently behave in a way that is inconsistent with how we perceive ourselves. And if we do not see ourselves as God sees us, then to that degree we suffer from a wrong identity and a poor image of who we really are. It is not what we do that determines who we are. It is who we are that determines what we do.[6]

Jesus himself said that truth is freeing (John 8:32). In a piece for *Harvard Business Review*, Robin Ely and her coauthors note that when women can transparently discuss the barriers present to their leadership potential, they are better able to navigate those barriers and lead beyond them. "They feel empowered, not victimized, because they can take action to counter those effects. They can put themselves forward for leadership roles when they are qualified but have been overlooked. They can seek out sponsors and others to support and develop them in those roles."[7] This kind of attitude is dependent on having a solid sense of self.

When we know who and whose we are, we will stop apologizing our way into the room and believe that we belong at any table to which we are invited. We will operate from a place of vocational strength.

I remember the day I finished an "I am" statement this way: "I am *an artist*."

It was a life-changing day. This thought came to me as new information. I've never defined myself as an artist, at least not consciously (I might have taken a hint from the fact that my own blog and podcast site is called *The Art of Holiness*). Now, to be clear, I don't paint. I don't do crafts. I don't play a musical instrument, don't dance, and am most definitely not a singer (lots of "amens" all around on that one). Still, *I* am an artist. This person writing this book! I am a writer, preacher, crafter of ministries and movements, creator of conversations and communities that welcome and advance the kingdom of God. What I failed to consider was *how* I approach all these parts of my vocation.

I am an *artist*.

Writing that statement for the first time in my life at the age of fifty-something, I was able to see my life and value in a whole new light. I sensed that maybe I even got a glimpse of what God sees when he looks at me. There was relief, a knowing. This life is not a mountain to climb but a canvas waiting to be painted. I am a cocreator with Christ in my life and vocation.

I *am* an artist.

No wonder I've been so frustrated by leading spiritually in a male-dominated work culture. In those early trainings, I was told that the whole point was to "get butts in the seats." I was given techniques to make that happen. For better or worse, the male-dominated world of ministry tends to emphasize techniques and methods, reflecting the priorities of an engineer, not an artist. I'm sure many men with an artistic bent share the same struggles I've felt in that world. Try as I might—mimicking their methods, using their mentorship, attending their seminars—I never quite got there. Even when I felt like maybe I was "getting it," it felt somehow less authentic, less true of how I'm designed to do this good work of gospel-sharing. Learning more about how I'm wired to serve and lead has been life-giving, fruit-producing, and anxiety-reducing. Surely that's true of both men and women. We all benefit from knowing what we're made for.

What Drives You?

There are two kinds of people in the world: people who like those little self-tests that define your personality in numbers or shapes or animals, and those who don't. Can I get a show of hands? Who among us is a fan of personality surveys? And who would rather cut off a finger than be forced into self-exploration? If you're the one running for a knife and trying to choose which finger you can live without, you're the one I want to talk to, because I get it. I'm a natural skeptic of sweeping generalities and tests that turn me into an otter or the color orange. I'm not a fan because we can rig a test to make it say whatever we want it to say. I believe we are fearfully and wonderfully made. God has embedded patterns in his creation. We know this by looking at patterns in nature. Clouds have types. Climates have patterns. Even wild animals behave in predictable ways. In the same way, people have patterns and categories that go beyond skin color and body type—patterns that are built into us, personalities and behaviors that are part of our created design. God is the author of these patterns, and some people have a gift for recognizing these God-given patterns and describing them so we can see them, too. Identifying these similarities can be helpful, not to paint people into boxes but to free them from unrealistic expectations.

The fact is, while we're all wired uniquely, we are not wired randomly, and there are a million ways to explore our very purposeful wiring. Beyond the "I am" exercise, I want to share three other tools that have been useful in my own journey toward knowing who I am in Christ. There are a million others out there, of course, so if these don't work for you, I hope you'll at least be inspired to go find some that do. Begin to explore your own identity in Christ. Let these tools stir up a conversation with God about who you really are.

The Enneagram

The Enneagram has become more trendy in recent years (and, as with just about everything, also controversial), but it can be a helpful tool for discerning how we've been shaped, particularly from the perspective of our weaknesses. It describes personality in terms of how we relate to God, others, and ourselves by beginning with the idea that we are all in recovery from our fallen state. We all operate based on lies we've been told about ourselves, and we all do things we wish we didn't (a malady from which Paul also suffered; read Romans 7). These lies generate what the

Christian tradition might term "besetting sins"—habits that keep us from God's best. The theory of the Enneagram is that we tend to overcompensate for these areas of weakness, and to the extent that we do, our personality is overworked. We all know people (or are people) who "present" with a mask on, as a kind of caricature of ourselves. As we come to understand our fallen tendencies, we can learn with the help of the Holy Spirit to rise above those compulsions, remove the mask, and surrender our identity to God. In Wesleyan circles (which happens to be my tribe), we call this the process of *sanctification*, and it is very much the process of unmasking ourselves so that our created design is exposed by the light of Christ.

As I mentioned, the Enneagram has no small number of skeptics and downright detractors, yet it has endured within the wider Christian community, particularly among mystics. Ian Cron and Suzanne Stabile give a hearty look at the history of this tool in their book *The Road Back to You: An Enneagram Journey to Self-Discovery*.[8] Cron's story of discovering the Enneagram particularly interests me, since it taps into the core theory of this chapter, which is that knowing ourselves can save us all kinds of grief and weariness in the quest toward effective ministry. He writes,

> For three years I tried everything short of surgery to transform myself into the kind of leader I thought the church needed and wanted me to be, but the project was doomed from the start. The harder I tried, the worse things became. I made more missteps than a guy running through a minefield wearing clown shoes . . . I thought about all the Bible teachers and pastors I knew who had done things that had blown up their lives and their

ministries, often on an epic scale, because they didn't know themselves or the human capacity for self-deceit.[9]

You may not be comfortable with the idea that serious progress can be made toward knowing who we are in Christ by beginning with our chronic or besetting sins, but admit it: Isn't this how all real spiritual progress is made? Doesn't it begin with confession? And as we confess our sins, he is faithful and just not only to forgive our sins but cleanse us from all unrighteousness (1 John 1:9).

The Myers-Briggs Type Indicator

The Myers-Briggs Type Indicator is another tool for providing insight into personality. Developed by Isabel Briggs Myers, this tool helps us orient around four general categories: introvert/extrovert, sensing/intuition, thinking/feeling, and judging/perceiving. I first engaged with this personality survey when I entered seminary and was surprised to find my introverted side. After years of being in public relations, a career that highlighted my gifts for public speaking and sales, I finally had language to define a hunger for alone time! As I've engaged with this tool in other seasons since, it has helped me understand how circumstances can emphasize and enhance the different parts of my personality.

Dr. Reg Johnson, who spent his career in the study of spiritual formation, has written a helpful reflection on the Myers-Briggs profile from a distinctly Christian perspective. He writes, "When we do not see our lives against the backdrop of the eternal God and the larger context of meaning in which He gives, our existence is constricted and centered basically upon ourselves. Such a narrow focus ends up corrupting life rather than enhancing it."[10] In other words, we do not engage in these methods of self-discovery in order to idolize the self but to understand ourselves in the service of a greater whole in which we all desperately yearn (whether or not we understand that yearning) to find our place.

Career Anchors

Career Anchors are one more practical tool that I've used in the Women of Worth ministry at The Mosaic Center. This is a well-worn tool, developed in the 1970s by Dr. Edgar Schein, a former business professor at the MIT Sloan School of Management. I like the approach he takes, because it fits with my own experience of needing to see the difference between technicians and artists. His inventory is designed to answer the question, "What drives you?"

Schein defines what he calls our vocational "anchors." These anchors are "a combination of perceived areas of competence, motives, and values that you would not give up; it represents your real self."[11] Think of this cluster of competencies, motives, and values as your nonnegotiables. Schein says that without an understanding of these core values, we'll find ourselves saying yes to opportunities that end up being a poor fit.

Schein identifies eight anchors:

- Technical/functional competence
- General managerial competence
- Autonomy/independence
- Security/stability
- Entrepreneurial capability
- Service/dedication to a cause
- Pure challenge
- Lifestyle[12]

What drives you—challenge or competence? Independence or dedication? For many of us in ministry, the drive may not match the resulting work. For instance, "Ellen" may have been deeply moved by the response of her community to her husband's death or her divorce. On the other side of that life-changing event, she may find herself increasingly attached to her faith community. She eventually begins to wonder if she can leave her own job and work full-time for the church. What Ellen doesn't realize is that being on the receiving end of pastoral care and on the giving end of strategic ministry development are two very different things, especially when it comes to how one relates to the community. When Ellen was the consumer of community care, she felt wonderfully connected to kind people. But when Ellen becomes the provider or developer of community care, she has to engage a set of skills she may not possess, not to mention a group of consumers who are now more demanding, less compassionate, and less connected than the community that nurtured her in her loss. Being on the receiving end of community care is a completely different dynamic than being on the vocational side of it; the latter can be wearing on a person, even if they are very much invested in the call. If they aren't invested, it is more than wearing. It is wearying and sometimes even devastating to faith. Understanding what drove Ellen to the call and what her anchors are might have saved her and everyone around her a lot of anguish. What are your anchors? What drives you?

I freely admit that it would be much easier to critique these or any other methods that invite a healthy amount of introspection rather than to engage in the hard work of self-discovery. After all, isn't this just holy-fied navel-gazing? Aren't we supposed to lose ourselves for Jesus? I would argue instead that until we make peace with who we are, we are incapable of getting beyond our "self." Consider this wisdom from Martin Luther's *Theologia Germanica* (via Reg Johnson):

> It may be commendable to ask, hear about, and gather information concerning good and holy persons, what they have done and suffered, or how they have lived and how God has worked and willed in and through them. But it is a hundredfold better that man deeply within himself learns and understands the what and the how of his life, what God is working and doing in his, and how God wishes to use him and not to use him.[13]

We all thirst to be seen, heard, and treasured. The One with the power to quench that thirst in us stands ready to reveal not just himself but us, too. After all, this same person he created is the one he has labeled "very good," from the beginning of time on the other side of Genesis 3.

Who Sees You?

One of my favorite names for God comes from the hard-to-hear story of Hagar, the servant of Sarai (before her name was changed by God to Sarah, and before she understood the significance of her own calling). In that story, Hagar is the tragic victim of an infertile Sarai's impatience with God's call on Abram's life. In her desire to see God get on with it and give them a family, she hands her servant over to Abram so he can have a child. After Hagar gives birth, Sarai becomes bitter and, eventually, kicks both Hagar and the child out of their home. Alone and desolate in the wilderness, Hagar prepares for both herself and her son to die. In that desolate place, God appears. He doesn't rescue Hagar from an angry master. He arms her with truth about his character. He is a God who sees us.

Hagar, an Egyptian slave, becomes the only person in the Old Testament to give God a name. Usually, it is God who tells us who he is as a way of helping us know who he is *for* us or what he plans *through* us. But here, Hagar is the one who names God.

> She gave this name to the LORD who spoke to her: "You are the God who sees me," for she said, "I have now seen the One who sees me." (Gen. 16:13)

The Hebrew term for "the God who sees me" is *El Roi*. It means both "powerful" and "God knows." This means that on the other end of a dysfunctional family conflict, God stands as the powerful One who knows Hagar, sees her, treasures her.

Somehow, that was enough for Hagar. She goes back into her work as one strengthened by "the God who sees me." She is known by God, and through that encounter, *she* now knows who she is, too. She is more aware of her purpose in the world, more sure of why she will return to a hard life full of uncertainty. She will go, because not only is she known, she knows. This is the real treasure of knowing our identity in Christ. When we know who we are, when we are comfortable in our own skin, we can enter into a world of uncertainty with an assurance that we are not in this alone. *El Roi* is with us.

CHAPTER 7

AUTHORITY

After You've Done All You Can Do, Stand

How would you finish this one-sentence prayer? *Lord, make me* _____. I ask because the last time I was in India, I had a prophetic moment around that one-liner that changed and challenged me. It happened one day when our team was doing some spiritual work with each other. I'd asked them to form a prayer beginning with the words, "Make me."

Make me empty, or *make me patient*, or *make me whole*, or whatever came to them.

As we went around the circle, each of us sharing our prayer and its purpose, every person on the team seemed to have recognized a strong sense of their need in the words they'd chosen. It was the same when it became my turn, though I was surprised by how viscerally I felt my response. I blurted out, "Lord, make me an elder!" Then, I burst into tears. As I sobbed (yes, uncontrollably sobbed; you're welcome, mission team), I heard myself say, "That is all I've ever wanted!"

Something inside me—it feels like it goes as far back as childhood—has always wanted to be a spiritual guide. I first sensed that call in a definite way when I was thirteen, so I've lived with this longing a long time. I want to participate in what God is doing in the world.

Not just participate. *Lord, make me an elder.*

Institutionally, I'm there. When someone in my denomination is ordained, the bishop lays hands on her and charges her with these words: "Take authority as an elder in the church to preach the Word of God, and to administer the Holy Sacraments." You and I both know that just because someone laid hands on you doesn't mean it "took." To become a spiritual elder is a very different thing than having a title or office conferred during a formal service. Becoming an elder is very much about *becoming.* Taking spiritual authority is a process, not a moment. Paul tells us (2 Cor. 4:16) that outwardly, we are wasting away, but inwardly, we're being renewed day by day. This describes the spiritual work of an elder—to be renewed, to be shaped and formed for the purpose of raising up another generation. Paul describes for Titus what that good spiritual work ought to produce—a leader who is blameless, faithful, not overbearing, not quick-tempered, hospitable, who loves what is good, is self-controlled, upright, holy, and disciplined (Titus 1:6–8). This is what it means to take authority. It isn't assuming a role conferred by contract. It isn't learning how to command the attention of a room or demanding respect. It is having the kind of character that *attracts* respect. Do you hear the difference? Think about Esther's story in the Old Testament. She had little to commend her as a potential queen, yet she "won the favor of everyone who saw her" (Est. 2:15). There is an element of favor in the recipe that produces authority. It begins with God. Spiritual authority is *spiritual*.

I regularly read a recovery-related blog called *The Small Bow*, and in a post titled "Learned Behaviors,"[1] the writer talks about Yashar Ali's rise to Twitter fame and subsequent crash. At the height of his popularity, Yashar had 772 *thousand* followers on social media . . . until he didn't. He was rated one of *Time* magazine's most influential people on the internet . . . until he wasn't. His problem was that he was too good at getting famous, exceptional at getting followers on social media, but rotten at generating substance. There was nothing to him except a guy who knew how to get noticed online. When that bubble burst, there was nothing left.

That's pretty much the opposite of spiritual authority. Spiritual authority looks like Paul's definition of love in 1 Corinthians 13—not boastful, proud, or rude; not demanding its own way. How do we "take" authority without *taking*? Without mowing people over, coming across as angry women or, worse, building a house of cards ministry and trying to pass it off as a mansion?

Remember that in part 1, we examined the legitimacy of a woman's place in ministry leadership. Believing her position to be authentic and of the Lord, we are now left to find our way to a place of sacred mastery over that glorious call and our own lives. If this is what we're after—not to command respect through bullying or illusion but to attract it by an authentically holy character—our next step is to learn what this looks like for *us* as individuals. What does "taking authority" look like in your skin, and how does that differ from what it looks like in mine? How do I wear this mantle of leadership so that I present an authentic version of myself? This begins with understanding how the process of taking authority differs for women and men, so let's talk about that.

Take Your Authority (Not His)

Here's a shocker: women lead differently than men. I'm not being completely sarcastic when I call that a shocker, either. It ought to be a self-evident truth (certainly by this point for any reader of this book), yet somehow it can still hit us as fresh information. Maybe that's because when it comes to our gendered differences, we seem prone to amnesia. And maybe *that's* because so many of our external influences are contrary to our own sense of what God is asking of us. Remember that we live on the post-fall side of Genesis 3, and the Enemy of our souls has a vested interest in keeping us off-topic.

The fact is, women understand power differently from men, and power wears differently on women than on men. For one thing, when it comes to taking authority, women tend to find their feet at different points in their development as leaders. Susan Vinnicombe and Val Singh studied what happens when women get leadership training designed with their tendencies in mind. They discovered that while men tend to develop autonomy and separation from others early on in their leadership journey, "it is only much later in their leadership development that women can tolerate separation and finally see themselves as equal to others."[2]

Women also tend to invite more folks to the table. Women's leadership authority tends to look less like "command-

and-control"[3]—in other words, less hierarchical and more collaborative. A *New York Times* article describing a study analyzing national political leaders discovered the following:

> Women tend to work more collaboratively even across the aisle toward consensus. In fact, the study showed women to be more effective at building coalitions and sharing power. Michael Genovese at the Institute for Leadership Studies (Loyola University) says, "Women share their power more; men guard their power."[4]

Alice Eagly, a professor of psychology at Northwestern University, studies and writes about gender and leadership. She offers three categories of leadership to consider: transformational, transactional, and laissez-faire. *Transformational* leadership "involves establishing oneself as a role model by gaining the trust and confidence of followers."[5] This style of leadership incorporates more mentoring, goal setting, and innovation. The focus is on the development of the next generation of leaders. *Transactional* leadership tends to focus more on the task by clarifying expectations, monitoring progress, and offering feedback, especially when correction is needed. *Laissez-faire* leaders tend to be more absent and uninvolved, especially at critical junctures.

Obviously, a transformational leadership style is more effective across the board. This style is more likely to attract, rather than command, respect. While both men and women are capable of achieving this style of leadership, Eagly's research shows that women not only tend to be more transformational in their leadership style but are more highly valued as leaders when they lead in this way. By "more highly valued," I mean that women are *quite* highly valued when they lead from an authentically transformational place. I'm not spouting anecdotal hopefulness.

Transformational leaders are willing to vulnerably share aspects of their lives beyond work. When their lives are seen within a larger context, they become more "human," and more trustworthy. In three different studies, women seemed more likely to be penalized as leaders (even as successful leaders) when they failed to communicate their experiences as communal beings—as people with relationships, who care for other people, people whose story demonstrates that others matter—while they were valued when they *did* communicate those facets of their lives.[6] Connectivity matters, and when women express their investment in others, it goes well for them. They gain the confidence of others, and become more trustworthy. The good news in this data is that women are wired for this. So why would we go to the trouble of imitating a leadership style that doesn't wear well when we may possess within ourselves a style that is highly effective and attracts respect?

This leads us to more good news. According to Eagly's study, not only do women tend to be more transformational (or collaborative) in their leadership style, they are better respected when they lead in this way. Eagly goes so far as to say that all things being equal, women have superior leadership skills because their natural inclinations tend toward more effective styles of leadership.[7] I'm not sure I agree with that or even want to (I count too many fine men of God among the leaders I respect and whose mentorship I appreciate), but I do appreciate knowing that when women lead from an authentic place, they stand a much better chance of being not just accepted but as effective as the men with whom they serve and lead.

One last bit of information to absorb: Eagly says, "The possibility that women and men differ in their typical leadership behavior is important because leaders' own behavior is a major determinant of their effectiveness and chances for advancement."[8] In other words, we can be our own worst enemies. When we don't recognize the natural differences in leadership leanings, and when we try to be something we're not in order to get along in a world we don't trust will accept us, we not only lose the best of what we have to offer, we also lose our sense of authority. Who can be confident as a leader when she isn't playing to her authentic strengths? Consider this from Vinnicombe and Singh:

> A consistent theme running through studies of women managers is the lack of confidence they show in themselves. They tend to rate themselves lower than male colleagues, and they have difficulty in accepting praise from others. This lack of self-esteem among women can lead to the so-called "impostor syndrome," in which women fear they will be found out or unmasked as unworthy of the success they have attained or the positions they have won.[9]

The moral is this: take authority—*your* authority. What I mean by "take" is *receive* the authority that has been freely given to you. Finding your own sweet spot when it comes to taking authority begins with knowing who you are in Christ. Start there. The sooner in your leadership journey you get to the work of exploring your own identity in Christ—knowing who you are, how you're made, what your gifts are—the more confident you'll be as a leader. As you take authority from that settled place, rejecting the inclination to constantly prove yourself, the more likely you are to attract the acceptance and respect of those with whom you simply want to share in the mission of God (make a mental note here; in a few pages we'll acknowledge that authority is given not just so we'll feel more comfortable but for the sake of those we serve).

Find Your Role Model

Find a role model. I'm not talking about finding a mentor (we'll get to that topic soon, though). I'm talking about finding someone after whose leadership you'd like to pattern your own, someone who can show you what your leadership can be. What are the qualities that show up in solid female leaders? What qualities show up in the leaders who resonate with you? According to Vinnicombe and Singh,

> Women value being seen as experts in their field, having an intrinsically interesting job, personal accomplishment, self-development and balancing work and personal life. In contrast, men see career success in terms of climbing ladders and gaining influence, with the external trappings of success including high salary, car and status. Given these different values, women are likely to approach their management education with different attitudes toward what is important for them in their path to leadership positions.[10]

Ruth Sealy and Val Singh also note that the lack of female role models is a significant challenge:

Our sense of what is possible in our careers is influenced by what has gone before, how we interpret that history, and how we draw inspiration and learning from leaders past and present in our own identity development . . . Role models are an important part of the development of social identities, and we argue, the scarcity of female role models in leadership positions plays a major part in the persistence of the gender stereotypical construction of leadership.[11]

It is vital to be aware of our preferences so that as we seek out examples to follow, we don't sacrifice authenticity in our quest for effectiveness. I wish I could get back all the time and energy I spent trying to implement everyone else's great ideas, all of which worked wonderfully in their churches and failed miserably in mine. I also grieve the lack of women in my life whose style of leadership and theological compatibility resonated with me, and who were readily available for conversation and coaching. It isn't too difficult to find people willing to give you an "attagirl." It's a true gift to find that rare person who is willing to challenge you at the deeper levels of authenticity and effectiveness. Because of this rarity, I have been most helped by the role models I have studied from a distance, whose biographies I've read, whose stories I've watched, whose lives attract my respect.

What about you? Look around the world—and around *your* world. Which female leaders inspire you? What specific traits seem familiar, like maybe you have those traits, too (or at least the potential to develop those traits)? Go back to your "I Am" statements, look for words that express leadership qualities, and then go looking for women who have them. Pray for God to connect you with the role model you really need. Ask yourself some defining questions, and journal your gut-level responses:

- What are your interests? What draws you to those interests?
- How have people in your life reacted to your interests?
- Have you ever felt different from others? When and how?
- Describe a time in your life when your concerns about how you would be perceived by others affected a decision you made, either online or in "real life."
- Who are the people with whom you can be your truest self? In what ways do they give you confidence to just be yourself?
- What are you passionate about? How do the things you are passionate about shape who you are?

Authenticity Matters

The 1995 movie *Toy Story*[12] is about the life and adventures of a roomful of animated toys owned by a boy named Andy. The boy's favorite toy, a low-tech cowboy figure named Woody, finds himself intimidated by a new toy in the room—a fancy plastic figure named Buzz Lightyear. The other toys are clearly impressed by this new toy with his lights, buttons, and wings, but Woody will have none of it. He wants the others to acknowledge what he knows: Buzz is just a toy and not a real intergalactic space ranger. Buzz, on the other hand, not only believes himself to be a real space ranger but expects his new friends to believe it, too. He even claims he can fly. Woody says he can't. After arguing, Buzz decides to prove himself. He climbs atop the bedpost and with his personal battle cry, "To infinity and beyond!" leaps into the air with every expectation that he will not fall but fly. What happens next is not flying, exactly, but it *is* impressive. With the help of a rubber ball, toy car, and model airplane, Buzz manages an airborne trick not even he could have manipulated. When he finally lands back on the bed, he proclaims a victorious "Can!" to enthusiastic applause.

Did Buzz actually fly? No. But he had the courage to make the leap because he believed that his abilities were cosmically conferred. This defines his personality. Throughout the movie, Buzz lives by a sort of self-fulfilling prophecy. Believing he is a real space ranger gives him the optimism and courage needed to attempt risky things.

Those who possess a high level of optimism combined with a deeply held sense of calling are the Buzz Lightyears of the ministry world. These effective leaders find themselves with a stronger than average sense of "Can!" Meet a successful female spiritual leader, and you will find someone who passionately believes in her work, is convinced it is both unique and important, and will gladly give her passionate "Can!" to see it succeed.

Authenticity is the "secret sauce" of effectiveness because it builds trust. When I talk about authenticity, I'm talking about knowing myself, my gifts, my limits, my life in Christ, and being able to live all of that out from a place of peaceful confidence. I'm not fighting for my place in the world, nor am I giving away pounds of flesh. I'm living what Paul might call the ambition of "a quiet life"—eyes on my own paper, working my own call, so that my daily life "may win the respect of outsiders and so that [I] will not be dependent on anybody" (1 Thess. 4:11–12). Paul isn't asking us to be quiet loners. Authenticity doesn't ask us to tamp down our passion or drive. It does ask us to actively seek sanctification in every aspect of our lives so we develop a mature connectedness that doesn't borrow unjustly from others' resources.

In their research on leadership, Steve Kempster and his team discuss two dynamics present in authenticity: "strength of identification with leadership role and fidelity to leadership purpose."[13] Both dimensions emphasize the importance of consistency in our inner and outer lives.[14] We don't have to put ourselves so far out there that we're fighting vulnerability all day, every day. Authenticity is about owning your role to the extent that you live it out with integrity. Transparency is about being honest within your role. It is about making sure your internals match up with your externals. Leaders possessing these dimensions create an atmosphere in which they and others flourish. However, this doesn't mean we must become so transparent that we're sharing thoughts or emotions that are not critical to the work.[15]

I want to share with you a bit of magic that will unlock your pathway toward a more authentic leadership style, but all I've got is this: stay after that sacred search for the treasure that is your identity in Christ. Go looking for the *imago dei,* the image of God that is within you. It contains a world of peace, an ocean of holy ambition, a mountain of quiet confidence. It is the headwaters of spiritual authority.

Go back to *Toy Story.* In the scene after Buzz Lightyear finishes his "flight," Woody takes offense. He announces to the stunned and impressed audience, "That wasn't flying. That was falling with style!" As their story continues to unfold, Woody and Buzz find themselves at a crisis point together on the wrong end of a rocket. The moment unites them. Exploding into the air, their sure demise impending, Buzz extends his wings and almost before they realize what has happened, they are flying—really flying. Woody exclaims, "Hey Buzz! You're flying!" to which Buzz exclaims, "This isn't flying. This is falling with style!"

This is a fair image of what authenticity looks like when women lead—when *anyone* leads. It isn't pretending to fly but leaping with hope. And when we find we can fall with style and enjoy the ride, even better.

Find Your Prophetic Voice

> The message that's really getting through to me these days is the whole idea that God knows me better than I know myself, and faith is believing that if I follow his lead, my true self will kick in where and how it's needed. I think, so often, I ignore or minimize experiences that tell me who I really am. I would rather find comfort at the current level and just stay busy. I really sense there is a lot more I can do.[16]

I wish I could tell you this quote came from a woman leader, but instead, it's from a man who came to Christ after living for decades as a practical (and kind of angry, at God at least) atheist. When he wrote this, he was discovering, much to his surprise and relief, that as he came to know Jesus, he was being birthed into a more authentic version of himself. Rather than experiencing religion as a restraining order, he found that life in Christ was characterized by rich potential. The Holy Spirit nudged him to dream God's dream for his life. He entered into the stream that runs through Abraham, Moses, the prophets, and untold others. Like them, he learned (and is still learning) that God majors in possibility and magnifies our potential.

> *I think, so often, I ignore or minimize experiences that tell me who I really am. I would rather find comfort at the current level and just stay busy.*

This revelation of a man seeking after God could just as easily be the collective voice of women who lead spiritually. We'd rather stay busy than do the hard work of excavating our more authentic selves. Can't we just organize programs, complete projects, check boxes, and feel good about what we've accomplished?

Friend, you have more than just good organizational skills, a pastoral heart, and the ability to multitask. God has more for you than just staying busy. You have a prophetic voice, and the world is waiting to hear what God would say—and would say through *you*. The result of embracing the image of God within us is the discovery of our unique voice, which God will use prophetically to speak his life-giving message into our communities. This is the prophetic edge of authentic leadership.

The gift of prophecy is the ability to see the world from the perspective of the kingdom of God (rather than the world) and to influence others by the way you speak into them. Joel teaches that with the outpouring of the Holy Spirit, God's people will begin to dream dreams, see visions and proclaim potential (Joel 2:28–29). This theme is echoed throughout Scripture. It is a call to see not only what *is* but what *can be*. Properly cultivated, a prophetic, visionary voice speaks life both corporately and individually. Every time a woman steps into the vision of Joel, she steps into that abundant stream that flows through our fathers in the faith, through Jesus himself, through this generation and on into the next as it heads toward the realization of the kingdom of God on earth. Larry Crabb brings this concept down to the soul level, asking,

> What would it be like if we had a vision for each other, if we could see the lost glory in ourselves, our family and our friends? . . . That power is the life of Christ, carried into another soul across the bridge of our vision for them, a life that touches the life in another with nourishing power. Vision for others both bridges the distance between two souls and triggers the release of the power within us.[17]

This is what the church of Jesus Christ needs most in this age. We need people who will confront sin, not from a soapbox but face-to-face in loving and redemptive ways. We need people who are not afraid to care for each other by speaking truth. We need people who walk out this life so fully that others are laid bare just by watching it. Women with a gift of pastoral care for souls have much to give the world through their prophetic voices. If we pursue a prophetic lifestyle, here's what will happen:

- We will have a heart for the ones who break God's heart.
- We will see people as spiritual beings and will look for where God is at work in their lives.

- We will learn to speak spiritually, which will lead us deeper into the heart of God.
- We will become hungry for the voice of God and will pursue his presence more faithfully.
- We will learn to appreciate the importance of holy imagination, which will cut through the debilitating sameness of life and infuse our daily lives with energy and creativity.

Discovering our voice not only makes us a better preacher, pastor, teacher, *leader*—it allows us to bring so much more to the table than simply a good mother's heart. The prophetic voice releases us from the tyranny of fear that drives us toward trying to control details—the place, they say, in which the devil resides. Fear tells us, whatever the challenge, that we are powerless. In our fallen need to control, we become hyper-focused on getting one thing right. The prophetic voice works to release us from that oppression, teaching us a new, more courageous way of living. It releases authenticity and authority not just into us, but into the communities we serve.

What if you learned how to listen to someone with one ear toward them and one ear toward the kingdom? What if you learned to elevate your thoughts above your circumstances to a level where you're looking for what God is doing? Begin by learning to speak words of blessing and encouragement as you pray over people. Prophetic thinking exposes us to the treasures embedded in other people. Paul says prophets speak to people for their upbuilding, encouragement, and consolation. That doesn't mean it will always sound like a fortune cookie ("You will make a change and your life will improve"), but we do train our inner eye to look for signs of hope in hopeless situations, to look for treasures in the messes around us, and to call out that which is not as if it is. That voice can be powerful, life-changing, even world-changing. Friends, never underestimate the power of a woman's voice to welcome and advance the in-breaking kingdom!

Taking Authority or Finding Favor?

What if the whole reason you are where you are is to participate in God's plan for his people? In other words, what if you have been shaped precisely for such a time as this?

That phrase, "For such a time as this," comes from the story of Esther, a Jewish woman crowned as queen of the Persian empire. Her story seems made for daytime television. Esther found herself in the royal palace at a pivotal time for the Jewish people—an awesome and humbling place to be, intimidating even. But there she was, in a place of influence at precisely the time when an official of the empire was finagling influence with the king so he could kill off all the Jewish people. Why? Because Esther's cousin would not bow down to him.

There was Esther, in the king's palace, with the king's ear, challenged to step up and lead in a time when her people were being oppressed and the leaders were not able to see the hand of God. Esther felt the weight and importance of her unlikely position, and even wondered if she was up to the task.

Then Mordecai, her cousin, sent her a word of advice: "Don't think for a moment that because you're in the palace you will escape when all other Jews are killed. If you keep quiet at a time like this, deliverance and relief for the Jews will arise from some other place, but you and your relatives will die. Who knows if perhaps you were made queen *for just such a time as this?*" (Est. 4:12–14 NLT, emphasis added).

In other words, what if you have been shaped into a person of influence and authority precisely for such a time as this? Perhaps God wants to do more through you and me than just help people feel better. Perhaps he wants to speak prophetically into the world, to reveal the overwhelming abundance of his power, wisdom, glory, and love.

God, forgive us when we have been content to offer to the world anything less than the beautiful witness of prophetic presence.

What makes Esther's story so powerful—and, by extension, the story of the Jews in her day—was just how unlikely a candidate she was to be a heroine. She was abducted from her home, placed in a harem, appointed queen when she had no credentials for it. Then, counseled by a cousin to stand up for their people, she took on the voice of a leader and stepped into power and favor from a place of quiet humility. "Queen Esther," the story goes, "wrote with full authority" (Est. 9:29).

The story ends as strangely as it began. The Jewish people are not spared from the fight. You'd expect that, but that's not what happened. They still had enemies, and they still had to prepare to fight them, but they were empowered by God himself. They prepared for battle, but as the story goes, "No one could make a stand against them." Meanwhile, Esther handled her moment with remarkable grace, courage, and wisdom. As I've said, *she took on the voice of a leader when she stepped into favor and authority from a place of quiet humility.* True authority is a potent force, and Esther teaches us some things about taking authority and attracting favor:

- Favor is about standing under the anointing of God. Authority is what we do with the favor we're given.
- Favor and authority come with an element of preparation and timing. This is a process, not a moment.
- Favor and authority are not earned or owned but shared.
- Favor and authority are not given for our sake but for the sake of people we serve.

Esther reminds us that when the authority is spiritual, the leader is willing, and the will of God is waiting, the world is deeply influenced for the good. Lord, make me an elder for such a time as *that*. And may all of us who hunger for our lives to count find courage to take the gift of authority given us and use it to share in the mission of God.

CHAPTER 8

EQUIPPING

Real-World Stuff Everyone Needs to Learn

If I were the person on the consumer end of this book, this is the chapter I'd have been waiting for, especially when I was young and in ministry. Back then, I probably wouldn't even have waited. I'd have skipped the other chapters, rifling through the pages in search of "silver bullet" advice. Never mind the woo-woo part about "finding your true self" or "becoming more like Jesus." The young-and-in-ministry version of me just wanted someone to tell me how to make my church work. Give me something I can *do*.

I'm writing this chapter on my fifty-eighth birthday, and I hope I've matured a little. I can say this much: the fifty-eight-year-old me knows what forty-year-old me didn't, that until I've done the foundational work of discovering my identity in Christ, of understanding what it means to take spiritual authority over my call, of making peace with the fact that I live in a fallen world, no amount of strategy will stick. Or worse, if it does stick, it runs the tremendous risk of wreaking havoc on my emotional and spiritual health, not to mention the health of those I serve. Therefore, this chapter is full of practical stuff I believe women need in order to make it work, but if you skipped the previous chapters to get here because you "just want someone to tell you what to *do*," that would be a lot like building a house on sand. Friends, the internal work is so important. Spend your energy building the spiritual and emotional foundation needed to lead in a fallen world, and you'll be much farther down the road toward successful ministry as you also learn the nuts and bolts of solid leadership.

Skipping the hard work of building foundational integrity so we can make sure the roof stays on is one kind of mistake in leadership development. The other kind of mistake is blindly assuming that a "me and Jesus" approach to church leadership is all we need. Let's review what we learned in chapter 1 from two significant studies by LifeWay and the Small Business Administration (SBA). LifeWay's study, conducted by Ed Stetzer and Warren Bird, focused on church planting in the US. One finding estimated that new churches tended to fail at a rate of about 32 percent after four years.[1] Meanwhile, a study conducted by the SBA discovered that among secular businesses, those surviving the first four years are still more likely than not to fail within the first ten.[2] According to yet another study by Mere Sovick, that very real risk of failure is greater for women business owners, who are roughly 10 percent more likely to fail than men.[3]

Because women are more likely to start a business with fewer resources at their disposal, Sovick concluded from his study that women leaders can decrease their rate of failure—or to spin it positively, *increase* their chances for success—by acknowledging the barriers they face and finding practical strategies to live beyond those barriers.

Stetzer and Bird reached the same conclusion for church planters in general (gender was not a category). They claim that "the chance of survivability increases by over 400 percent when the church planter has 'realistic' expectations of the church-planting experience."[4] As we said in chapter 1, what is true of church planters must surely be true of leaders in general. Ministry leaders are more likely to survive when they know what they are getting into and how to navigate the challenges.

In the world of computer coding, there is a thing called a naïve algorithm. It is an oversimplified answer to a complex problem. When a coder finds one on the way to building a program, it can seem like a great fix, an elegant and creative solution. Best of all, it's easy! The trouble with a naïve algorithm is that while it begins simply enough, over time it creates more and more complexity, consumes more and more time and memory, and is ultimately quite inefficient. The real telling is in what happens over time, because the gaps don't show up immediately, but they do show up eventually. The valuable and imminently transferrable lesson is this: "It's better to be simple, slow, and understandable than complex, fast, and difficult to grasp."[5]

In other words, knowledge is power, while naïveté is dangerous. The idea that good intentions, a good heart, a love for people, and faith in Jesus will invariably lead to ministry success is not just naïve but dangerous. Of course, we want our leaders to have a solid spiritual foundation, but how much better it is if they also have a toolbox of best practices from which to build an effective ministry! This was my driving question heading into this project:

> What tools and training can be placed into the hands
> of women called to lead so that those who hear
> that call have every resource at their disposal?

What do women (and men who support them) need to know so they are strategically equipped for real-world organizational leadership that is transformative? Where are the educational gaps? What assumptions do we need to voice, then intentionally build from?

I suggest an emphasis on focused, professional training in at least these four major areas:

Fund Development and Management
- Training in how to negotiate terms
- Training in fund development

Leadership Development
- Training in leadership development
- Training in team-based leadership

Vocational Development
- Training in identifying the right situation for each skill set
- Training in identifying effective coaches and mentors
- Training in networking

Personal Development
- Training in time management and life rhythms

These areas of focus aren't randomly chosen but derived from dozens of personal interviews with women leaders as well as a deep dive into multiple academic studies. I encourage every female leader reading the following pages to ask where her own gaps are in these areas. Let this conversation inspire you toward further reflection and study. I am convinced that we who lead are called, as we said in the introduction, to be as "wise as serpents" in our pursuit of effective leadership (Matt. 10:16 ESV). So let's dig in.

Fund Development and Management

I want to start with the most difficult topic first because I believe that confidence in this area will lead to confidence in other areas of leadership. I believe women have been short-changed (no pun intended) in their training for financial leadership. Here's my advice: don't let training in the area of fund development and salary negotiation intimidate you. Here's a fact: Nonbelievers know it takes money to run a ministry. Believers know it takes money to run a ministry. And everyone knows that the worker deserves her pay. People are not put off by discussions of practical things. To the contrary, I believe they starve for it, and for the theological underpinnings that make things like giving make sense. I believe folks are generally starving for compelling reasons to follow Jesus more sincerely, and as spiritual leaders, it is our responsibility to make that happen. Discipleship gets real when we begin teaching and training in the area of money. If we're not comfortable ourselves when addressing these needs, our folks won't be, either. Giving, like any discipleship issue, requires education, and that begins with its leaders.[6]

Training in How to Negotiate Terms

Back in chapter 1, I quoted a leader whose comment still resonates with me. "Do I deserve a raise? Hell, yes, I deserve a raise," she said when asked about how her church was faring financially. "But I know the church can't do it. And you know, a man might just make it happen, but I can't. I negotiate myself out of it, right?" If a man "might just make it happen," what makes that leader think she can't? Why do we self-sabotage when it comes to equitable compensation? Sometimes it's because we fail to call out the faulty logic ("Your husband makes plenty, and the church is struggling. Why are you asking for more?"). Sometimes it's because our care for people collides with our leadership gifts ("I know how hard my people work and how little they make. How can I ask for more?"). Finally, sometimes it's pure passive aggression ("Why should I have to ask? Why don't they offer what they know I'm worth?").

That last excuse? That's just plain naïve. *We* are our biggest problem. We tend to undervalue our earning power. Author Barbara Stanny (now Barbara Huson), in her study of high-earning women, writes that women tend to glamorize low- and no-pay positions and have a high tolerance for low salaries and financial chaos.[7]

None of these motives are legitimate, and none will allow you to receive what you need in order to invest where you're serving for the long haul. Nor will these faulty motives help your congregational leaders to care maturely for the work of the church. Also, please don't assume you'll "just know how" to negotiate a salary when the time comes. Harvard Law School offers a whole degree emphasis on negotiation research, much of it focused on how women negotiate.[8] (This tells me that it takes an advanced degree to get good at negotiation!) Go back to our chapter on perception as a barrier to understand why this is harder for women than men. Assertiveness in women is often seen as negative, and negotiation is usually seen as an assertive practice, so we back off. Professors at Harvard Business School confirm this double bind once again:

> Eight years after Sheryl Sandberg encouraged women to persevere on the corporate ladder in her book *Lean In*, critical obstacles still stand in the way of gender equity, particularly when it comes to pay and promotions. Based on the results of [a study by Professor Julian Zlatev and colleagues] . . . negotiation dynamics not only contribute to the dearth of women in leadership roles, but also create a lose-lose situation for all women in the workplace, as neither assertiveness nor conforming to stereotypes leads to success.[9]

Obviously, you need more than a paragraph to figure out how to become a better negotiator when it comes to both salary and budget increases, but let the advice in this paragraph suffice as encouragement to go looking for great resources to enhance your style of negotiation and financial goals so that you don't end up doing your job from a bitter place. As Leslie Knight says, "Focus on the result. Your salary, your lifestyle, and your perceived value are your responsibility."[10]

Training in Fund Development

"I am not a natural fundraiser," admitted one leader. "I avoid the 'ask.'"

We all do. The "ask" is not our default setting, mostly

because we're afraid of it (see the above conversation about negotiation). And that's mostly because we don't truly understand the power of our own stories. I remember Gordon Cosby, longtime pastor of the Church of the Saviour in the DC area, once telling a group that if a ministry is struggling financially, it may be God's way of encouraging its leaders to go out there and "tell the story"—meaning they should view their financial need as an opportunity to get into the community, raise awareness about their ministry, and ask for support. To Cosby, this was just another way to spread the gospel. All fund development is, in the long haul, is raising funds and developing donors for good ministry through the process of *de*fining and *re*fining vision, of telling and retelling our stories, so that every person God has gifted with a call and passion for this work might be uncovered and activated.

Learn to tell the story of this ministry to which you're called, and learn to share your vision at the drop of a hat, because those are the things to which people give. They give to compelling stories and visions. People do not give to needs or deficits. (Isn't this good news? You never have to talk again about what you *don't* have!) This is especially true of people who have learned to manage money well. They have no desire to pour their money into a sinking ship, but they will give in places where they see God moving.

I can say with complete joy that Mosaic Church in Evans, Georgia, would not be alive and vital today if it were not for generous givers beyond our local congregation who have continued to pour out year after year, especially in the early years of our development, simply because they believed in the vision. Our top external giver lived in another town, visited our building only once, and never set foot in our worship service. But year after year, he gave generously (as much as $100,000 in one gift) with one request: "Send me the stories of transformation." Upon his death, I was deeply moved to remember how his faithfulness to God's call to give generously was, for us, among the most beautiful means of grace.

We have also learned how to access grant funds, and through those funds, have built things like accessible indoor and outdoor play areas for kids with special needs. We've learned that every giver has more than one pocket, and targeted marketing can help connect those who care with the projects they care about. As I've said on my own blog on the topic of fund development:

> At the end of the day, another person's giving is not about funding your ministry (or helping you sleep at night). It is about following Jesus and inspiring others to do so. Our main work is not to develop givers but to develop disciples. And according to our Scriptures, healthy, committed disciples will be compelled to give.[11]

Fund development both within and beyond the congregation is essential to growing a congregation. For women, it is critical to the flourishing of ministry. Go back to chapter 3 and our discussion on limited resources as a barrier when women lead. As one leader said, "My inability to draw and sustain a crowd . . . correlates to the giving needed to sustain a worshipping community."[12] Let this both inform and motivate you to seek out training in fund development. If you don't know where to begin, start with an excellent resource by Thomas Jeavons and Rebekah Burch Basinger called *Growing Givers' Hearts*. Trust that

God has a vested interest in equipping those he has called so they can fully participate in the welcome and advancement of God's kingdom.

Leadership Development

Our church was founded at a time when marketing to gather a crowd for a "launch service" was the prevailing approach. That is how I was trained, so that is what I did. All my energy in the early days was focused on that first service. I didn't stop to consider just what I would do with people when they showed up. When I realized I'd need some kind of system in place to help us retain those who came to that first service, I quickly recruited a few small group leaders and gave them the titles of a few of my favorite studies. With that amount of preparation, we launched about ten small groups. Against all odds, those first groups managed fairly well, providing at least the appearance of spiritual care and connection for most of the adults in our new community.

Ironically, the relative success of those first groups worked against our long-term growth. Because we had the "problem" of discipleship and connection "solved," I moved on to other things and never took the time to develop a more mature and integrated system of active connection. As a consequence, our growth stalled when those early groups stagnated, and when they eventually died, there was no leadership pipeline in place to replace them. Since then, our small group system has undergone several more near-death experiences on the way to being finally systematized for sustained growth. We learned the hard way that solid systems and leadership development are critical to healthy community formation. I now emphasize leadership development and team-based leadership in every area of our church's life, and it has made all the difference in our ability to sustain ministry.

Training in Leadership Development

Cultivating the leadership potential of others means understanding (1) that women may attract more "potential" leaders than seasoned leaders, and (2) that our own style of leadership may be an acquired taste. Knowing who we are and how we present as leaders within this process is yet another gift we give the body of Christ. Trisha Taylor, a family systems thinker and leadership coach, has reflected on the challenge of finding our own way of being authentic while honoring others who think differently. "I don't know how we grow that capacity other than doing it, reflecting on it and walking through the discomfort and the pain of it and then doing it again," Taylor writes. "Except, I would add, we commit to do this work in community with others who are on the same journey."[13]

Doing it, reflecting on it, and walking through the discomfort of it is a poignant description of my own journey into self-discovery as a leader and systems developer. I've had great coaches along the way, though almost all of them have come to me through the books they've written. *The Leader's Journey* by Jim Herrington, Trisha Taylor, and R. Robert Creech is a strong, insightful look into Bowen's family systems theory and its connection to congregational dynamics. *Doing Leadership Differently* by Amanda Sinclair has been an incredibly valuable resource that includes some barriers and strategies to female leadership not addressed in this book. *The Fifth Discipline* by Peter Senge is a significant study on systems thinking. Frank Viola's *Finding Organic Church* speaks to that hunger we all have for developing not just systems but "unforced rhythms of grace" (Matt. 11:28–30 MSG). Kevin Watson's *The Class Meeting* helped shape our community toward discipleship and away from programming, a model that works well for me, as a female who's more gifted at cultivating community than drawing a crowd. I have also used coaches and have a networked group of leaders I tap regularly for help in developing our church's leaders. I recommend you gather a similar group of unpaid consultants for yourself and let them challenge you toward developing systems that grow healthy, long-term leaders.

Training in Team-Based Leadership

Especially in the early years of planting a new congregation, I found myself jealous of my male colleagues who serve large churches with staff teams. They have people who can share the load—full-time associates who collaborate on all aspects of ministry, including preaching. I'd find them on Facebook, high-fiving their staff members for a sermon well-preached, and I'd secretly covet what they had. I'd catch them on Twitter as they described amazing team meetings where groups of enthusiastic staffers white-boarded brilliant ideas. I'd read their posts, attempt to suppress my envy, then return to my solitary work of building systems, building sermons, building a church.

That was my practice for the first fourteen years at Mosaic. Then, I had an encounter with the Holy Spirit that changed everything. I was given a vision for building a preaching team using the gifts of people already in my congregation. In the span of a minute or two, the Lord showed me four lay people who were already part of the church who could be gratefully cultivated as regular preachers. What has happened since that vision has been one of the most refreshing, renewing opportunities in my ministry. Raising up a team of preachers who share the load has addressed some very basic needs in our ministry. And I love coaching a new generation of preachers! Not all of my team are folks who plan to become pastors. Two of them have jobs they also enjoy (both are experienced teachers, as it happens), and to which they also feel called. They have not been called to pastor, specifically, but they *do* have a gift for preaching. Sharing the journey with them has brought fresh energy and inspiration to my own gift. I love meeting with them to talk about the art of preaching, and I love coaching them on the back end of a message to help them hone their gift.

I feel like the man who found a treasure buried in a field. When he found it, he went and bought the whole field (Matt. 13:44–46). In the formation of a preaching team, I have found a treasure and, within it, a plethora of benefits. This is just one example of how training in leadership development can reap profound results, give breathing room to a spiritual leader, and unleash the whole people of God for the whole work of God.

I'm convinced that building teams is crucial to the work of building strong churches. Read David Shenk in *Creating Communities of the Kingdom: New Testament Models of Church Planting* for practical reasons why teams are an essential piece of community formation. There are so many good reasons to get specialized training in team-based ministry. Teams ensure the viability of ministry areas. If a ministry belongs to a team and not a person, then when one person needs to drop out, the whole ministry doesn't die. Teams grow leaders and uncover talent. Teams keep the workload and decision-making of ministry from "flowing up." That is, the decisions and work are accomplished as close to the ministry as possible, rather than higher up the organizational ladder. Teams prevent burnout. And teams appeal to anyone who has the gift of collaboration. If formed well, teams present a balanced, diverse face for the ministry.

Did you know there are reportedly tribes in South Africa who typically use the greeting *sawu bona,* meaning literally, "I see you"? The common response to that greeting is *sikhona*, which means, "I am here." This exchange is the product of a worldview that understands that until you see me, I do not exist. In other words, we exist *only* as we exist together. We belong to one another, and our spiritual gifts are activated most effectively within a community built on team-based ministry.

Vocational Development

Here's a cold, hard fact: no one is going to advocate for you, your gifts, or your circumstances quite like you will advocate for yourself, your gifts, and your circumstances. This means that knowing what you're wired for, what your limits are, and what you're willing and able to do becomes critical to your ability to stay in this good work for the long haul. (This, I hope, is what we all want; no one goes into ministry expecting to burn out, right?) While we've talked a lot about knowing who we are in Christ and understanding our gifts and call, we also need training so we can continue to develop that call in each successive season. Otherwise, we will allow ourselves to be placed in unreasonable places for the sake of fulfilling the goals of others.

Don't expect someone else to know what you're capable of, and don't expect them to act unselfishly on your behalf. Yes, friends, even in the church, folks act selfishly and without transparency, and they also act pragmatically without the church's best interests in mind. I've been in too many rooms where people approved someone for ministry who wasn't ready, reasoning, "Well, if not them, then who?" That "who" doesn't have to be you if you're not up for that particular challenge, as long as you understand yourself well enough to know what you're wired for, what your limits are, and what you're willing and able to do. Then you have the right—and perhaps the obligation—to say no to an invitation you know you're not up for. Keep in mind what those LifeWay and SBA studies revealed: we do better when we know better. Just understanding our circumstances makes a tremendous difference in how we navigate them.

Training in Identifying the Right Situation for Each Skill Set

I'm thinking about a woman I once hired to be an administrative assistant. I'd known her before we hired her, and I was particularly impressed with her flawless ability to remember every birthday, anniversary, and special event in my life. She even remembered the anniversary of my mother's death, and she had never met my mother! She not only remembered all these special occasions, but she sent cards. Inside the cards, she included little handcrafted magnets with Bible verses tailored to both the person and the occasion. She did this not just for me but for dozens of people, maybe a hundred or more. I have no idea how she kept up with it, but I was so impressed with her system that it didn't even occur to me to question her organizational abilities when she applied to be our administrative assistant. I figured someone with that kind of card-sending track record would be an organizational whiz and would quickly pick up whatever skills were necessary.

I was dead wrong. As it turned out, that precious woman had two great skills—remembering dates and sending cards. She was in the ninety-ninth percentile among all humans in the world for those skills. But administrating anything else? She was lost and very quickly became miserable working for someone who was frustrated by all we couldn't accomplish together. Mercifully, we parted on good terms, but I learned a valuable lesson from that experience. It is dangerous to set people to work that is outside their anointing or gifting. It is also dangerous not to know your own anointing or gifting, because then you will agree to do things you're incapable of. For that reason, we need training to identify the right situation for our own skill set. We need to know ourselves well enough that we won't say yes because of flattery heaped on us by someone with an agenda, nor will we let ourselves tolerate things that take up our time and keep us from flourishing.

How can you learn the right situation for your skill set? I encourage you to begin with tools like the Myers-Briggs personality profile and Edgar Schein's classic *Career Anchors: Discovering Your Real Values*. I've gotten a lot of help from coaches (both formal and informal), and I suggest a good bit of research before you commit to a professional coach. Like therapists, not all coaches are created equal. The people we surround ourselves with are such an important piece of the puzzle that I'm going to save the topics of training in identifying effective coaches and mentors and training in networking for the next chapter. I believe the benefits of good coaching and building a strong network are huge, and I'll say much more about these topics in the following pages. For now, let's turn to one more important area of equipping women to lead.

Personal Development

Susan Vinnicombe and Val Singh have contributed much to the conversation about what happens when women lead. They advocate for women-only training opportunities, not exclusively, but as part of a total training strategy, because their studies indicate that women benefit greatly from opportunities to be with other women in leadership roles.[14] Such opportunities allow women space to clarify how they feel and respond to their work roles, and they provide opportunities for conversation about experiences unique to women who lead. Power dynamics and politics can be unpacked "in a safe environment in which they can test their own experiences against the experiences of other women."[15] Most importantly, women can discuss lifestyle issues connected with leadership, assessing areas where further planning, training, coaching, or therapy might be helpful.

Training in Time Management and Life Rhythms

In all my conversations with female leaders (both within and beyond the church), no other subject was mentioned more often—usually in an exasperated voice—than time management and life balance. Women often feel the strain of multiple roles more acutely than men and find themselves struggling to grasp that elusive thing called "balance." I've already tipped my hand on this subject.

In chapter 5, I mentioned that I think balance is a myth and that the quest for it tends to produce more guilt than peace. But I also get that saying this doesn't fix anyone's chaotic life. To figure out what you need in this regard, I suggest a life coach who will ruthlessly work with your calendar. I can tell you that personally, I've never been helped by someone telling me to "do less." I *have* been remarkably helped by a coach who paid attention to my time, who taught me how to use a calendar to schedule not just meetings and events, but the prep work involved in getting them ready. Cal Newport's *Deep Work: Rules for Focused Success in a Distracted World* as well as *Digital Minimalism: Choosing a Focused Life in a Noisy World* were both life-giving for me, literally. The concepts in these books gave me big chunks of my life back.

Before you blame the world for not giving you enough time in the day, get honest with yourself about where you are now in your personal and spiritual life. I'm sure I'm not the first to say that healthy people develop healthy congregations, and healthy congregations develop healthy people. That's the goal—that you and those you serve will not fall exhausted across the finish line but will break through the ribbon joyfully, "feeling God's pleasure."[16]

March On, My Soul

Deborah, that Old Testament judge/prophet/warrior, was such a beautiful mix of wisdom and calm-but-not-quiet strength. Deborah was unafraid of a good challenge, or of standing shoulder-to-shoulder with men. She spoke with candor and courage to the men with whom she was in partnership. Deborah was fearless, with a passion for truth and justice. It is clear from her song in Judges 5 that it never once occurred to her to be embarrassed or intimidated by her own place as a leader, warrior, prophet, and champion. Her spirit in the face of challenge was captured in her simple yet powerful battle cry, found in Judges 5:21:

March on, my soul; be strong!

How strengthening that call is! How encouraging!

Stay the course. Lean in when it all seems too daunting to tackle. Don't let threats or pressures push you around. If you've been called to this, march on and be strong.

What a rugged and robust call for those of us who are preparing to lead: *March on, my soul! Be strong!* I hope you will hear it as God's word for you if you find yourself wearied by the task of adequately preparing for ministry. I also hope you will let Deborah's voice inform yours as you hold in tension both the practical and prophetic sides of this good work to which you've been called.

The fact is that all the practical training in the world comes to nothing if it is not built on the foundation of solid spiritual anointing, and Deborah models that for us. When she stepped onto the platform of strategic leadership, she was coming out from under a tree, where she'd been practicing for years the prophetic discipline of listening to the voice of God. Her example reminds us that training will take us only as far as our spiritual sensitivities have been honed. In other words, if you really hunger to lead spiritually, and if you want to make the most of the training in which you invest, then learn to listen for the voice of God. Eagerly desire the gift of prophecy, as Paul counseled

(1 Cor. 14:1–4). Knowing how to form teams, design systems, negotiate salaries, and balance time is important for effective ministry, but knowing how to discern the voice of God is the difference between life and death for anyone who follows Jesus.

Whatever else you can commit to from the ideas offered in this chapter, I encourage you to become hungry for the listening side of prayer and for prophetic wisdom. The promise is this: that as God finds you faithful to sit beneath the palm of Deborah—learning his voice, channeling his wisdom—he will be faithful to show up and pour into you. You will begin to hear things that sound smarter than anything you could have thought of yourself. You will begin to develop hungers for specific areas where God is working—maybe in a life, or a situation, or an area of the world. You will begin to bear supernatural fruit in this good work you've been given, fruit that will last (John 15:16).

I get very excited thinking that there are Deborah spirits reading this right now who are ready to do battle with the Enemy of God. I love knowing that God is raising up a generation of women who are wise, calm-but-not-quiet, unafraid of a good challenge or of standing shoulder-to-shoulder with men. I am exponentially energized by the notion that if God wants a woman to lead an army against the darkness, he'll have an army of strategically equipped and willing women from which to choose. With that vision before me, I can confidently sing Deborah's prayer-song:

May those who love you rise like the sun in all its power! (Judges 5:31 NLT)

Yes and amen. March on, my soul; be strong.

CHAPTER 9

PARTNERSHIP

Why It's Okay for Men to Open Doors

Men and women are created for partnership.

Take a minute to absorb this statement. Notice everything about how you react to it. Does it seem logical? Does it chafe against your worldview in any way? Do you consider this to be an affirmation, or is it a dangerous idea for you? How does your mind work to fit this concept together with what you've been taught, whether formally or informally?

Now, read it again:

Men and women are created for partnership.

I hope by this point, we've examined the topic enough that you at least see the logic in the above statement. The question is, do you believe it?

I'm sure I don't have to tell you that there are plenty of places in the world where this *is* a dangerous idea, places where it is either illogical or outright heretical to say that women and men are equals in the work of spreading anything, much less religious truths. But let me tell you why *not* believing in and trusting this statement, even in this country, is a dangerous idea.

It is dangerous, first of all, because if this statement is true, then ignoring it is rejecting God's design. Ignoring this truth limits the options and potential of women and men who have resources and experience to offer the body of Christ. It limits churches that are starving for gifted, trained, mature leaders. To ignore or disclaim this creation story truth is dangerous to the spread of the gospel and to the church of Jesus Christ. It hits the mute button on the prophetic word of Joel, discounts the experience of the apostle Paul, and minimizes the realities of first-century Christianity.

Why would we do that? To avoid the "danger"? To play it "safe"—or what, on the surface, masquerades as safe? How much better for the body of Christ when men and women both seek to maturely reach for their creation call and enter the work of ministry seeking only God's best for his bride. Friends, I believe it, have staked my life on it, and am convinced of this freedom-generating truth:

Men and women are created for partnership.

We've come full circle, from building a theology rooted in creation story partnerships (see chapter 1), to being able to think practically about how that theology plays out in the real world. This is where we get to dream together—men *and* women, laypersons *and* clergy—about the good work of opening doors, mentoring, coaching, networking, co-laboring. Let's talk winsomely about how to offer all these resources to gifted women in an era when too many have been paralyzed by a culture that has defaulted to fear rather than calling adults into spiritually and emotionally mature partnerships. The goal of this chapter is to get us beyond frustration and moving toward solutions that unleash the fullest potential for advancing the kingdom of God. We will talk briefly about two distinct tools: mentoring and coaching. Then we'll shift to a discussion of the benefits of both male and female mentors, coaches, and trainers. We'll explore the gifts of advocacy and networking and how these strategies can level the playing field and enhance opportunities for collaboration, team building, and door opening. What a privilege it is to offer the world a winsome witness of what is possible when we reconnect to the creativity of God and the partnership for which men and women were designed. Let's get started.

Coaching, Mentoring, or Training: What Do I Need Most?

Anyone can benefit from mentoring, coaching, and training, but of course, our purpose here is to discuss how women, specifically, can benefit from this kind of support. For our purposes, coaching "develops self-awareness and self-reflection" as it relates to a person's vocational gifts and call.[1] Think of a coach as an objective voice focused on maximizing professional goals. Mentoring is defined as a career development tool that offers "informed support and understanding" within a particular context.[2] Mentors tend to focus more holistically on developing the thought processes of a leader. Think of them more as advisors. Training focuses specifically on the development of gifts and may also be used to advance specific accreditations, such as counseling, chaplaincy, or financial guidance. Think of training as skill development more likely gained in a workshop or classroom setting, while coaching and mentoring—designed to create paradigm shifts—are more likely to occur one-on-one.

What is the difference between a mentor and a coach? Think of a baseball pitcher. The *coach* is there to achieve specific, observable goals by turning the pitcher's potential into reality: getting the ball over the plate or throwing from the stretch. He's honing specific skills. The *mentor*, on the other hand, is there to develop more abstract, inner qualities by guiding the player's journey from insecure rookie to confident veteran: bouncing back from a slump or handling the stress of a long season. Both the *coach* and the *mentor* have a relationship with the player, but the coach's focus is on the nuts and bolts of technique—on getting the job done—while the mentor's focus is on the architecture of the whole person, on helping the pitcher become a seasoned player and steadfast teammate. One is there primarily to coach potential into reality and achieve specific goals. The other is there to set the next generation within the context of the grand game.

In the end, the distinctions are not as important as the recognition that all three—coaching, mentoring, and training—can greatly enhance a leader's effectiveness. So which one is best? The answer—wait for it!—is *yes*. All three have their place. The biggest mistake I've made in discerning which one I need at any given time is that I often wait until I'm desperate to go looking for help. Then I too quickly settle for the first willing person I find. While it is true that crisis is often the more effective catalyst for change,[3] I'd like to help you avoid my mistake of waiting for the disaster to strike before you get motivated. There is wisdom in being more thoughtful and proactive when it comes to getting the support we assuredly need to succeed in ministry. We've already devoted a chapter to the kinds of training that might best help women acclimate to and excel in lead roles. Now, let's spend a little more time discussing the advantages of coaching and mentoring.

Coaching

Coaching has become increasingly popular these days—it seems like everyone wants to be one or have one. There are all kinds of coaches—fitness coaches, life coaches, performance coaches, faith coaches, you-name-it coaches—and you may discover that you need help in multiple areas, not all of which are directly related to your day job. Through discernment, you may discover that you need to begin not with a coach but with a therapist. The difference is in the inner work you want to emphasize. Do you need to process what has already happened in your life, or do you need help shaping a vision for what is ahead? Even reading this book may have uncovered some uncomfortable feelings related to your own place as a leader, and if so, you may need to take time to explore with a therapist where those responses are coming from. But if the questions arising from this study leave you hungry to know more about how to move forward from here, you may be best helped by a coach.

What I want you to hear is that a coach is *not* a therapist. A coach's role is to help you integrate your skills, gifts, call, and work so that you're able to maximize what you bring to the table vocationally. Tony Stoltzfus, a coach for coaches, defines it this way: "Coaches are change experts who help leaders take responsibility for their lives and act to maximize their own potential."[4] Timothy Gallwey, a coach for athletes, describes it this way: "Coaching is unlocking a person's potential to maximize their own performance. It is helping them to learn rather than teaching them."[5] Taking time to reflect, pray, and evaluate your priorities for growth will help greatly in discerning which kind of coach you need. Don't skip this step. Get as many thoughts and questions down on a page as you can, so you can begin to see patterns in what is taking up your mental space and where you need to focus instead.

Mentoring

Mentoring focuses more on the relationship than on objective goals and is meant to be a journey. It is what connects us from generation to generation. David Clutterbuck's extensive studies of coaching and mentoring help to distinguish mentoring as apprenticeship, "when an older and more experienced individual passe[s] down his knowledge."[6] Coaching can happen within a staff team. Mentoring is probably best reserved for a relationship beyond the day-to-day work world (although, certainly, there are no absolutes here), where we are free to explore in a more holistic way the life experience of both mentor and protégé.

Jorge Acevedo, a colleague whose modeling has shaped my ministry profoundly, describes the work of mentoring both men and women into ministry:

> A quarter of a century of ministry in the same community has taught me that there seems to be a broad and diverse process by which women and men are mentored into ministry. First, they are discovered. Some wise,

Spirit-led person taps an unsuspecting follower of Jesus on the shoulder and says, "I see something in you." The sensitive spiritual leader has a kind of "radar" that spots potential spiritual leaders and seeks to join the Holy Spirit in "calling them out." Second, these "called-out" potential leaders are developed. They have reported to me, "You gave me a challenging task that I was sure I could not do." Leading a mission team or giving a talk at our recovery ministry have been confirming experiences for these younger and newer leaders. Third, these now called-out and confirmed leaders are commissioned by the church. They are "set aside" for the task of a ministry. Sometimes, this has meant formal credentialing through our denomination, and other times, this has been an elevation within our local church to an assignment (joining the staff) that does not require credentialing. Currently, the Grace Church operational team is made up of two women and two men. Together, they lead the four campuses and many ministries of our church. The two women on the team were discovered, developed, and deployed "from the chairs of Grace Church." The other male on my team has been mentored by me for more than thirty-seven years, beginning when he was in high school. Regardless of gender, spiritual leaders are charged with calling, confirming, and commissioning women and men to join Jesus in his mission. This is the work of spiritual leaders.[7]

Space and time don't allow us to go beyond describing the differences between coaching and mentoring. Mostly I want you to hear the difference (and that there *is* a difference) so you can better discern which is more useful to you right now. If what you need at this moment in ministry is someone to help you articulate your potential, deficits, and goals (and how to address each), then a coach is your best bet, one chosen to target your specific area of need. If what you need is the slow drip of wisdom from someone who has been where you hope one day to be, then you would likely benefit from a mentor. In fact, I'd argue that you need both at any given time in your ministry, but the greater wisdom here is to use discernment and intentionality when choosing who those coaches and mentors will be. Toward that end, I'd like to say more about what men and women each bring to the table in the work of coaching, mentoring, and training.

Woman or Man: Which One Do I Choose for Support?

In my surveys of women leaders, I noticed that most had no mentor speaking into their lives, and that those who did were more likely to have male coaches and mentors.[8] That teaches me two things. The first is obvious: there are a lot more men in ministry than women. Second, to the extent that men decline the opportunity to mentor/coach/open doors for women in ministry leadership, women are left with few choices.

The good news is that most women leaders with whom I talked who had male coaches rated their coaching experiences as positive. This tells me that coaching of women by men can be done, and done well, when healthy boundaries are in place. What mattered most to those women was the quality of the support, not the gender of the one offering it. As one leader said, "I sought a mentor not based on gender but on excellence."[9]

What do women leaders gain when they seek out the coaching, mentoring, and support of other women? And what do they gain when they seek out the coaching, mentoring, and support of men? How can we best help women to get the most benefit from outside support so they can lead effectively?

When Women Mentor Women

Let's begin with the unique gifts that women leaders can offer other women leaders. Throughout this book, we've taken the position that women lead in ways that are different from men, and that there are leadership challenges unique to their gender. If that's so, then it makes sense that there are ways women might uniquely benefit from the shared experience of other women. Consider these results of a survey by Nicole Williams, who works with LinkedIn:

- Fifty-one percent of women between eighteen and twenty-nine years old (Generation Y) surveyed by LinkedIn noted that they are being or have been mentored by women.
- Forty-three percent of women between thirty and forty-four years old (Generation X) noted that they are being or have been mentored by women.
- Only 34 percent of women between forty-five and sixty-six years old (baby boomers) noted that they are being or have been mentored by women.[10]

It may be that younger women have more female mentors at their disposal than earlier generations, but it may also be that we are slowly acknowledging the value of gender-specific mentoring and training. In fact, some business schools are beginning to tailor women's courses to meet their specific needs. Susan Vinnicombe and Val Singh have studied the dynamic of mentoring and training among women in business, and they acknowledge that women are not only challenged to find qualified mentors but may be misunderstood when they seek out the professional support of men.[11] For some women, it may be more effective to seek out exceptional "women-only" trainings where "the emphasis is on helping women managers to help themselves become more effective."[12] Without apology, these kinds of training opportunities are designed to challenge women to succeed without compromising their own styles of leadership, by offering coaching or training in networking, mentoring, negotiating, and other tools. What do women-only programs offer that mixed-gender training can't?

Perspective

Antoinette Alvarado discovered in her study of women leaders that women who make use of female mentors have a greater ability to succeed as leaders.[13] There are some things only women know or learn about leadership, since they have experienced what they've learned *as women*. Those experiences are like gold for other women who hunger for help wading through options to find the right leadership framework for each stage of their lives.[14] Women who lead as parents at various stages may better understand the life rhythms of a mom, passing along valuable perspective on time management and holy rhythms.[15] Women may benefit greatly from a place where they can discuss with other women how to handle the stress and pressure of ministry life. Women may need opportunities to learn professionally from other women, not to quarantine them from "the big guys," but to give them space and experienced voices they can hear and learn from. Vinnicombe and Singh note that "it is valuable to provide women with their own forum in which to discuss what stresses them, the consequences of their stresses and how they handle stress."[16]

Vulnerability (Less Tension)

Because women can often hear the voices of other women more clearly and less defensively, vulnerability is another benefit of gender-specific mentoring and coaching. For women, connection often (not always, but often) trumps information.[17] Connection requires vulnerability, and vulnerability is easier to achieve without the tension of gender-related dynamics.

Modeling

Imagine just how much we could expand the imaginations of young women if we could expose them more regularly to effective female leaders, especially those in larger contexts. Role models are an organic way to impart vision and inspiration to others. And role models are an important way that we move beyond gender-bound stereotypes[18] and expand our collective imagination when it comes to leadership in the church.

Wisdom and Experience

There is nothing quite like being in the room with someone who really "gets" you and who can speak to your experience from a place of personal understanding. You'd think we'd have lots of opportunity to seek one another out and get the encouragement we need, but so often, women in male-dominated professions tend to get spread thinly across the organization (often in order to have their representation as broadly noted as possible) and end up separated from each other.[19] That leaves them with little room to hear and learn from other female voices. We hunger for spaces where we can interact not just socially or therapeutically but *as professionals*, sharing wisdom and experience and encouraging one another toward our best.

When Men Mentor Women

In my surveys, I discovered that women want coaches who understand their context, and they clearly value effectiveness over gender when seeking out a coach. Four out of five had the experience of a male colleague helping them to achieve their goals, acting as a door-opener when they sought a position or opportunity.[20]

It is clear that women have much to offer other women. But if we settle for grouping all females together, or pairing women only with other women for coaching and mentoring purposes, we miss so much opportunity for growth and creativity. I'm not only thinking about how men can help women, but also about how women can help men. I currently coach two young men in different areas of ministry, even as I am coached by men who have much to offer me vocationally. Let's talk about the benefits of being coached or mentored by men. What can men offer women in the way of perspective, experience, and, perhaps most importantly, door-opening?

Perspective

Often, women leaders are working within a church culture that has been dominated for decades by male voices and ways of leading. Some of the best wisdom men can offer women is that of perspective—understanding this culture and how best to respond to it. Again, let's turn to the insight of Vinnicombe and Singh:

> A key issue arising in women's management programmes is women's interaction with organisational politics and personal influence . . . For many women managers, as in their definitions of career success, the focus at work is task accomplishment, challenge, high standards, expertise and attention to detail. They do not see the relevance of politics. They feel that if they are good at their jobs, others should notice and promote them. They should not have to make themselves visible, promote themselves or network with senior managers to build sponsorship.[21]

Some women will flourish in a competitive or politically thick environment. Others will appreciate coaching in how to acculturate to these dynamics and learning effective strategies to navigate them.

Door Openers

Door-opening, or sponsorship, can backfire when we become too eager to promote women or men without clearly understanding their potential. That for me has been one of the more frustrating aspects of promoting women into leadership roles. In our overenthusiasm for seeing women serving at all levels of leadership, we have too often promoted women who aren't equipped for or even interested in the assignment they've been given. It's important not to shy away from opening doors but to prefer an organic approach to a programmatic one.[22] Women benefit greatly from learning to assertively ask for an open door in areas where they need it. A woman might start as a small group leader, move into a staff position as leader of small groups, progress to congregational care, and over time, find that she really enjoys leading other elders and take on an executive pastor role. Likewise, men benefit from consciously remembering to bring others with them when they walk through doors into new opportunities.

One of my most important discoveries has been realizing that male colleagues often have connections that can open doors I might never have been able to open myself. I've received great help from men who have introduced me to funding sources, talked me through coaching options, and recommended me for ministry opportunities. You wouldn't be reading this book right now were it not for J.D. Walt (who calls himself "the chief sower" and visionary for Seedbed, a publishing house in Nashville, Tennessee), who first opened the door of publication for me and invited me to walk through it. Without his advocacy, my publishing story would have been very different. I've also been greatly helped by men with personal access to larger donors and have learned to ask for what I need. Another leader shared a similar story: "Grant funding from the community was often initiated or supported by male colleagues—some clergy, some laity."[23] I have discovered among my colleague-friends that most are very willing to help, but understandably don't have my needs in mind unless I voice them. Who on your short list of friends and colleagues may have access to resources or information that could move your ministry forward?

Networking: The Exponential Effect of Partnership

Finally, let me say a word about the exponential value of networking, a practice we can all embrace. Do you remember Heidi Roizen's story from chapter 2? Her secret to success was her remarkable ability to network within and beyond her "mission field," which was Silicon Valley. Networking, simply, is about building relationships, and it plays into the gift of collaboration many women carry. Networking generates possibilities in all the areas we've discussed in this chapter and the previous one. As we cultivate relationships, we open ourselves up to others who carry gifts and graces that will only enhance our ability to do ministry.

Mentoring and Coaching Across Genders: Is It Safe?

Maybe you've heard about the "Billy Graham Rule."[24] For the uninitiated, the Billy Graham Rule was so coined after Graham made the public commitment to never meet alone (in a car, restaurant, hotel, or office) with a woman other than his wife. His was a high-road choice to avoid the rumors swirling around other national leaders of his generation. Martin Luther King Jr. and John F. Kennedy, both contemporaries of Graham, battled their own demons where sex and women were concerned. Graham didn't want to fall into those same traps. I commend Billy Graham for making a strong statement about his personal boundaries. I would say that for him, as a very public figure, it was the right choice. He was a target, and his public declaration put the world on notice.

Since his "rule" became famous, scores of Christian leaders have taken the same tack as Graham. Many have accepted it as a clear and easy way to avoid temptation or even the appearance of it. For some, it is the right choice, given their personal challenges (either internal or external). But is it the right choice in every instance, just because it was the right choice for one high-profile man?

A *Washington Post* editorial by Laura Turner spells out the nuances for both men and women of invoking this rule:

> The impulse that led to the Billy Graham Rule—which was actually a solidification of principles guarding against several kinds of temptation—is a good and honorable one: to remain faithful to one's spouse and to avoid the kind of behavior (or rumors of behavior) that have destroyed the careers of church leaders. Evangelical pastors having affairs is so common as to almost be cliché, and damages the integrity of the church.
>
> But good intentions do not always produce helpful consequences. In this case, the Billy Graham Rule risks reducing women to sexual temptations, objects, things to be avoided. It perpetuates an old boys' club mentality, excluding women from important work and career conversations simply by virtue of their sex.[25]

The question is one of how both men and women leaders can live irreproachable lives while raising up those in their spiritual care. What is the right balance to strike? And what is the real issue beneath hard-and-fast rules like Graham's?

In a word, it's about holiness. How we live out our lives before Christ so they bear fruit for the kingdom is the real issue. But it is also about healing. Let me reiterate the importance of healthy interaction between men and women in leadership roles. When we address our own brokenness and face our own prejudices and feelings of inadequacy, then and only then can we effectively live out our own call to raise up others.

My friend, Bryan Collier, is a good example of someone who has intentionally worked to find a healthy way to mentor across genders. Bryan's church (The Orchard, in Tupelo, Mississippi) has been a role model for my church since the day it opened its doors. I became a student of his work from afar, then literally became his student when I pursued a doctorate at Asbury Theological Seminary. Bryan has been a solid advisor, friend, door-opener, and supporter of me and our ministry. Because I know the journey he has made, from restricting his mentoring relationships to male-only to making space for mentoring men and women, I wanted him to share with you directly what that journey was like for him, and how he now processes his own contribution to the ministry of women leaders:

> I really overreacted for the longest time to mentoring a person of a different gender than me, erring on the side of caution (you know—the Billy Graham Rule). However, one day I realized that gender was the least concern I should have when considering a mentoring relationship because the characteristics that made for a good/healthy/ productive mentoring relationship were true no matter what gender I might be mentoring. Likewise, the characteristics that made for a bad/unhealthy/unproductive relationship were true regardless of gender. So I refined my criteria a little bit by thinking through it more holistically and began to say yes, regardless of gender, when

these characteristics were in place: (1) Their primary relationships (family, spouse, work) were healthy. They weren't dependent on me to bring or coach them into wholeness in these areas. (2) Their spiritual maturity was substantial enough and evident enough to bear the weight of the task or area they were asking me to mentor them in (for example, I won't coach a church planter who isn't spiritually mature enough to plant a church). (3) I was the best person for the mentoring role (i.e., I couldn't think of anyone who might be a better fit for their request or would help them progress much better). (4) I could connect them to other resources or resource people in the area of requested mentoring (i.e., I wasn't being asked to be the lone expert in an area or they just wanted to work with me). (5) They were willing to join "group think" with other people I was connected to who might be working on the same issue or pursuing vocational growth in the same area.

Having said all that, I want to emphasize that mentoring someone is a deep engagement on my part. It seems inauthentic to work vocationally with someone so intentionally and yet stay detached from their personal and family life. When we do ignore a personal interaction, it ignores the fact that we are multidimensional beings. It pretends that one area of our lives doesn't affect every other area. That simply isn't true. So while I would say I don't want to bear the burden of bringing emotional and relational health to someone, I do want to be able to engage with them around their primary relationships. In my mentoring relationships, I am interested always in how it is with their soul, their primary relationships, and their work. But that means I need to know something of their relational dynamics. With that in mind, I always ask about their family by name, and I always talk about myself in the context of my wife and family. Especially in mentoring relationships across genders, I believe, setting ourselves in context reminds us that the mentoring conversations that we are having are just part of our lives, which encompass so many more people, responsibilities, and opportunities.[26]

I appreciate how this leader challenged himself to objectively think through and find pragmatic ways to shepherd the whole congregation in his care. Rather than limit his access to other people, he increased his access to the Holy Spirit and, with careful discernment, found a solution that would work for him.

A Few Questions for Men

The work of finding creative and healthy ways to raise up the next generation of leaders, so that this gospel which has been entrusted to us is passed on, is the responsibility of every spiritual leader. With that in mind, I want to pose a few questions for men, especially (although I absolutely believe women must also find peace with mentoring, coaching, and training across genders). As you meditate on these questions, spend time discerning where you may need the guidance of the Holy Spirit to move forward:

- Do fear or immaturity have a voice in the choices you make around hiring, mentoring, or encouraging women?

- When you consider mentoring, coaching, or supporting women in ministry, do you notice any emotional triggers rise to the surface? Have you followed those triggers to their source?
- Do your decisions give women access to all areas of leading and serving in the church of Jesus Christ? Where are women excluded?
- Do your decisions reflect the values and spiritual maturity of an elder in the New Testament church of Jesus Christ?
- Have you learned the differences in leadership styles between men and women, and are you able to appreciate and support those differences?
- Are you in any way stifling the advancement of the kingdom because of your own (perhaps subconscious) discomfort with working collaboratively with women?
- Do you know how to say "no" (or sometimes, "not yet"), when someone is not spiritually prepared for the work of ministry?

In some ways, we're now concluding the most important chapter, because unless we learn to live out the other nine chapters in partnership, we've gained nothing. If, after reading all this, we turn to women leaders and merely say, "Man, you've got a steep mountain to climb, but thanks for marching on, and good luck with that!" then we've added nothing to the conversation except another interminable level of victimizing. The whole point of this study is to get beyond what we cannot control so we can strategically focus on those places where we can contribute. And that word is for all of us—women and men.

Men and Women Were
Created for Partnership

The last scenes of John's gospel relate how Jesus restored Peter to his calling. He used a combination of grace and vision, moving Peter beyond his past mistakes and speaking a mission into his life: "Feed my sheep" (John 21:17). Peter pays this forward in an often-overlooked scene in Acts 9, when Peter is called to the house of a young woman who has died. Peter is sent to the room where her body lies. When he gets there, he gets down on his knees to pray. Then, he calls out her life. "Tabitha, get up," he commands. And she does! Peter takes her by the hand, helps her to her feet, calls for the believers, and presents her to them alive (Acts 9:40–43). When Tabitha is raised up, her story is told all over town, and many believe in the Lord. In this story, Peter calls Tabitha a "disciple" of Jesus. It is the only place in the New Testament where the feminine form of the Greek word for "disciple" is used.

This resurrection is the third in a series of stories in Acts 9 where people are "raised up" in various ways. Tabitha's story teaches us that the call to "rise up" is not just for our own sake, but for the cause of the kingdom of God. Is there any better mental image for what coaching, mentoring, door-opening, networking, and training can do for a life? It can literally be the difference between life and death in a ministry.

When God's people get serious about their faith and begin acting on it, not only are we raised up, but other people are raised up, too. People are saved. People are healed. People are called out by God to do great things. People finally figure out how to welcome Jesus into their hearts.

In *The Message* version of Paul's letter to the Colossians, he includes a challenge that seems remarkably relevant to us as we press into becoming all we were meant to be and do:

> So if you're serious about living this new resurrection life with Christ, *act* like it. Pursue the things over which Christ presides. Don't shuffle along, eyes to the ground, absorbed with the things right in front of you. Look up, and be alert to what is going on around Christ—that's where the action is. See things from *his* perspective.
>
> Your old life is dead. Your new life, which is your *real* life—even though invisible to spectators—is with Christ in God. *He* is your life. When Christ (your real life, remember) shows up again on this earth, you'll show up, too—the real you, the glorious you. (Col. 3:1–4 MSG)

The real you. The glorious you. That's what we're *all* after. May it be so in your life and mine.

CHAPTER 10

IT'S ALL ABOUT THE KINGDOM OF GOD

We began the second half of this book with a quote from *Good to Great* by Jim Collins. He says that when what you are good at comes together with what you are passionate about, "not only does your work move toward greatness, but so does your life."[1] The church of Jesus Christ has reached its quota of leaders who are underprepared, underqualified, and undermotivated for the challenging work of kingdom building. Ministry leaders who are deeply passionate about fulfilling Jesus's prayer for the kingdom to come aspire to greatness—for his sake—and they ought to have every resource needed to do the work well. Likewise, women who hunger to be spiritually influential leaders—who long for something more than the status quo—deserve the resources to become exceptional.

Consider this: faith traditions that affirm the place of women in ministry are inviting us to become privileged investors in a global movement. As one denominational leader told me, in some places, such traditions will be the only ones who can employ women in the whole nation or region.[2] Isn't that exciting? Do you understand the potential of our collective witness? When what we are good at comes together with what drives us as a movement and what sets us apart theologically, then we bear the seeds of greatness and the potential for a global renewal. Stop and consider the magnitude of this fact. Traditions that allow women to lead have twice the resources at their disposal as traditions that do not. We can place tools and training into the hands of women called to the ministry. We can design strategies to help women leaders discover and develop their unique leadership styles. We can shift the conversation from what is wrong with women in church leadership to what will release the massive leadership potential present in our gender.

Friends, what if the kingdom of God is straining toward the day when *all* God's people are deployed in the work of the Great Commission?

Among my dearest partners in mission is a couple who serve an evangelistic ministry headquartered in an Asian country currently under increased persecution. They are passionate about sharing the gospel among the least-reached tribes of their home country, and they often say they believe their nation will be won for Christ by its women. Given the treatment of women in this culture, that statement feels like an unlikely ideal, but they train evangelists and see amazing things happen among women all the time. One such woman of God, whom we'll call Suraya (not her real name), bolsters their hope in this prophetic vision. Here's her story:

Suraya was raised as an outcast in her country and in her religion. She was poor from the day she was born with no way to escape. When she married (to another outcast), she and her husband sold moonshine to make ends meet.

Then, one day, she met a Christian who told her the biblical story of the Samaritan woman. She listened as this believer related the tale of an outcast woman who was forbidden from using the town's well when other women were there to draw water. She heard about how Jesus talked to this woman and took a cup of water from her while he told her everything there was to know about herself. Suraya heard the story, went home, and wrestled with it all night long. The next day, she went and found the person who'd shared the tale and asked them to tell it again. A few days later, she eagerly asked again to hear this story. After hearing it for the third time, Suraya said, "I want to be part of that story." She came to believe in the saving grace of Jesus Christ because he related to a woman like her as if they were living on the pre-fall side of Genesis 3.

In Suraya's part of the world, indentured slavery is still very much a reality. People like her who have a lot of debt can sell themselves to a rock-busting company or to some other form of hard labor, and the owner of the company will pay off their debt. But once they are "owned" by that company (or that person), it is almost impossible to win freedom. Suraya and her husband ended up enslaved by their debts and doing hard labor every day. Then my missionary friends met them, heard their story, and decided to buy them back.

Now, Suraya travels all over the region preaching the gospel of Jesus Christ. My friend says she goes places he would never go, and she preaches boldly, trusting God to not only protect her but to amplify her voice. She doesn't have a Bible because she can't read. But she knows the stories, and she knows the gospel. So this beautiful woman of God tells the stories of Jesus and plants churches in parts of the world that are starving for good news about redemption and restoration. As of this writing, she has planted twenty-six house churches and supervises dozens of pastors. She has no resources, but Jesus is her doctrine, and his stories are her gospel.[3]

Isn't it exciting to think that in some of the most difficult spiritual ground, new growth is springing up? Isn't it even more exciting to think that it is happening through a female voice? Beautiful things can happen when women lead. The Lord is going to keep doing new things in ways that seem illogical to us, because his people keep praying for the kingdom to come, and this is how the kingdom comes. It comes when we reject the lies of a fallen world, learn to treat one another as God designed us, and release the whole people of God to go and make disciples.

In our Bible, there are many examples of women who were raised up into positions of leadership: Deborah, Mary, Priscilla, Lydia, to name just a few. Meanwhile, the cultures of religious traditions without these kinds of examples reflect deep inequities. Some years ago in India, a few hundred girls went through a renaming ceremony. These girls all carried the Hindu name *Nakusa*. It means "unwanted," and it is a common name among girls in India. Someone decided to issue an invitation to girls carrying that name, offering them the chance to choose a new name. Literally hundreds of girls showed up for that ceremony—girls tired of being called "unwanted."[4]

The widespread oppression of girls, found in so many cultures across the world, reveals the sinfulness embedded in our unredeemed human nature. Females are made to feel like runners-up in the gender contest. This is not a Christian teaching. Paul said, "Christ has set us free to live a free life. So take your stand! Never again let anyone put a harness of slavery on you" (Gal. 5:1 MSG). As followers of the gospel of Jesus, we believe everyone is wanted and gifted in some unique and treasured way for sharing the good news. As another of my heroes, John Wesley, founder of the Methodist movement, famously said, "God owns women in the conversion of sinners, and who am I that I should withstand God?"[5] Indeed. Who are we that we should hamper the spread of the good news about Jesus?

Tim Tennent, president of Asbury Theological Seminary, teaches us that the missionary task is bigger than we tend to give it credit for. It is not only teaching or preaching—as important as those tasks may be—or discipling or training, or even evangelizing. Along with those activities, one more component is vital: cross-cultural transmission.

Tennent writes, "When we see the church being planted cross-culturally, we begin to see that the gospel is being brought to new people groups, and that is the missionary task." And why is that distinction important? Because, Tennent says,

> Even if every Christian in the world became an evangelist, and they witnessed to everybody they knew, and everyone they knew became Christians, and they themselves became evangelists, even after you had tremendous movement to Christ all over the world, there would still be over a billion people who had never even heard the name of Jesus. Why? Because they had no friends or neighbors to evangelize to them, to speak the Word of God to them. So however vibrant the church's life may become in various parts of the world where the church is planted, however vivacious the people's witness may be,

however mature the church's growth, the world will not be reached, the Great Commission will not be fulfilled, until people cross cultural barriers and bring the gospel to those who have not heard it.[6]

This is precisely why Paul's "Macedonian vision," in which the Holy Spirit called him across the sea and onto European soil, is so important to this whole conversation about unleashing the whole people of God to share the whole gospel of God to the whole world.

We tend to blame Paul for much of our angst surrounding the conversation about women in ministry leadership. Quoting 1 Corinthians 14 and 1 Timothy 2, we discount any evidence of Paul's partnership in the gospel with women and throw him under the bus. I would urge against that tendency and commend Paul to you as both a door-opener and a true advocate.

Begin with Acts 16, where Paul stands at the edge of Asia Minor, at that time the farthest frontier of the evangelized world.[7] He and his companions are in Troas, [having] traveled throughout the region of Phrygia and Galatia, having been kept by the Holy Spirit from preaching the word in the province of Asia. When they came to the border of Mysia, they tried to enter Bithynia, but the Spirit of Jesus would not allow them to. So they passed by Mysia and went down to Troas. (Acts 16:6–8).

Due to the lack of an open door, Paul is left to wonder what in the world God is up to. Here is this type-A, git-'er-done apostle trying to win one for the kingdom, begging for an opportunity to do what he does best while God seems to be closing every door. Paul's fixation on the known territory of Asia distracts him from God's heart for *the rest of the world.*

This kingdom-generated frustration feels like the equivalent of bumpers in a bowling alley. The Holy Spirit is keeping Paul in his lane, nudging him toward the coast where he will finally be able to gaze across the Aegean Sea toward Macedonia and everything beyond. The story goes on, in Acts 16:9–10:

> During the night Paul had a vision of a man of Macedonia standing and begging him, "Come over to Macedonia and help us." After Paul had seen the vision, we got ready at once to leave for Macedonia, concluding that God had called us to preach the gospel to them.

There Paul stands, at the far edge of the gospel—perhaps the only follower of Jesus bold enough to push open the gate to the global West so the rest of the world can be introduced to a global Messiah.

Come over to Macedonia and help us.

So they begin to travel through Macedonia, stopping in Philippi. Here's what happens next:

> On the Sabbath we went outside the city gate to the river, where we expected to find a place of prayer. We sat down and began to speak to the women who had gathered there. One of those listening was a woman from the city of Thyatira named Lydia, a dealer in purple cloth. She was a worshiper of God. The Lord opened her heart to respond to Paul's message. When she and the members of her household were baptized, she invited us to her home. "If you consider me a believer in the Lord," she

said, "come and stay at my house." And she persuaded us. (Acts 16:13–15)

Paul has not only opened the gate for the gospel to flow into Europe, but he has also widened the gate for women to hear the gospel and *lead in advancing it*. In this one prophetic act, he has introduced the gospel to the global West and also crossed back over to the pre-fall side of Genesis 3. By doing so, he opens the door for Lydia to join a fellowship of biblical women who dare to walk back into the unspoiled garden of Eden. In a profound way, I owe my own life and call to this scene with Lydia, and to Paul's boldness. How radical of this first-century follower of Jesus to sit down and talk with these women outside the city gate as if they deserved a fair account of the gospel right alongside their brothers and husbands.

This scene places Lydia alongside all those other women honored by Paul in Romans 16:

- Phoebe, a deacon in the church
- Junia, outstanding among the apostles, imprisoned for the faith
- Priscilla, a coworker in Christ
- Mary, who worked very hard for the community of faith
- Tryphena and Tryphosa, women who worked hard for the Lord
- Persis, another woman who worked very hard for the Lord
- Rufus's mother, who was a mother to Paul, too
- Julia and an uncounted number of sisters, and all the Lord's people who were with them

It is stunning to note how many women are mentioned by Paul in this one chapter! How can we see him as anything other than an advocate and a partner in the gospel? For me, this section of Romans rivals the "Hall of Faith" in Hebrews 11 in its significance as a witness to the world of what can be and as an encouragement to women who lead. In my estimation, Paul is *for* us, not against us. By leaning in and caring actively for the role of women in church leadership, we prove our brand of egalitarian theology. We collectively determine that we will not be so pragmatic in our pursuit of church development that we leave women behind. By unleashing the whole people of God to share the whole gospel of God, we more fully cooperate with Christ in welcoming and advancing the kingdom of God. Above all else, this is our goal.

What a glory to note how God is using women to lead in powerful movements around the world. The evangelistic explosion being documented in Iran even now is largely due to the leadership of women.[8] Missionaries in India tell of the critical role of women in introducing the gospel to new groups. I believe it is our turn, and I am passionate about equipping a generation of women to rise up with tools in hand to welcome and advance God's kingdom on earth.

Felicity Dale asks a poignant question: "There have been times when everyone knew God did not want women to lead in the church. Could there be a time when everyone knows the opposite is true?"[9] The first-century church proved that when men and women work together to build the kingdom of God, operating in freedom and in the power and giftedness of the Holy Spirit, the effects of the fall are reversed, and the glories of the gospel are exposed.

And After We've Done All We Can Do . . .

Some time ago, I got an emotionally charged email from a frustrated female leader who had taken one too many hits. Never mind what had happened to her that day to unleash all her pain and anger. Suffice it to say that she was *done*. She was writing me to find out if she could quit. That almost-weekly desire to quit is not exclusive to women pastors; all sorts of ministry leaders—both men and women—go there. But I recognized the tone of this woman's email. I'd been right there so many times. I also knew that what she needed most was not permission to quit, but permission to *feel* on the way to persisting. So here's how I responded to this sister in need:

> Friend,
>
> I hear your pain. I am so sorry for it. I suspect you already know the stuff we all know—that we live in a fallen world, that we aren't going to be able to make partnerships out of hierarchies again until we are all back on the other side of Genesis 3, that "standing" in the Ephesians 6 sense of that word is hard as heck but still the best option and offense we have in a fallen world.
>
> After we've done all we can do, we stand. That's the call.
>
> And standing can be tiring. Holding an uncomfortable position can be uncomfortable. And yes, it can get old, and after enough of it, we would rather just do our small work and grow old and bitter than keep pushing against the boulder. That's our choice. But that's not the call.
>
> The call is to stand. After we've done all we can do, stand.

So go ahead and blow off some steam and be angry and sound off, but then get back at it. Get back to making your stand. Learn winsome ways to make your point, and stay in the game. The call doesn't disappear, and it is so much more frustrating to avoid a call than deal with the pressure inside of one. Stay in it. Stand.

Be angry at injustice and at the Enemy of our souls who has found a foothold in gender inequity, but don't assume we can win that argument and defeat human fallenness—that somehow, if we just say it right, the thing will go away. This is human fallenness we are battling. It is in our DNA. Be angry about what the Enemy has done to humanity, but don't settle for the cheap way out by blaming Hollywood or government or men in general. Make sure your arguments are biblical, theologically sound, and practical.

This thing we deal with is a thing that won't disappear in an instant, so how do we navigate past it so we can do the things we're called to? How do we as women support each other without competing or belittling or forgetting? How do we raise up men by encouraging them to love and respect us as colleagues and sisters in Christ, without competing with or belittling them?

They say we are 400 percent more likely to succeed if we know what we are up against. So here's what you're up against:

Sometimes you will experience condescending attitudes from men who have no idea they are being condescending.

Sometimes you will experience the jealousy of women who have no idea they are broken in that way.

Sometimes you will experience subtle and even overt

sexual advances by men who know what they are doing and by men who got broken as boys.

Sometimes you will be passed over by churches because you are female, because people are gripped by the spirit of fear.

Sometimes you will be invited to speak/sit on the platform/write/participate precisely because you are female (take it—every time, take it; never mind their motives).

Sometimes you will experience a lack of success because you are female, and sometimes because you're not that great a leader. It will be hard to know which is which.

Sometimes you will feel crazy because when you verbalize your experience of any of the above, others will deny or minimize what you're feeling. They'll tell you you're doing "just fine." You will feel crazy because what you know to be true is not validated.

All these things will happen to women who choose the path of leadership. Hundreds of studies bear out the fact that you will have at least some combination of these things in your life. This is not to say men have no challenges of their own. Men have other things to deal with (and some of them are very difficult), but these are *our* things.

So now you know, which means you are now 400 percent more likely to succeed. If you will accept that we live in a fallen world, that you may not be able to fix all these things, and that God would rather you spend your time and energy on something other than being angry about these things, you will do well. You'll find the humility to stay under the Lordship of Christ.

If what I'm saying here doesn't settle well with you, then do your own research. Find your own message. But whatever else you do, don't let unholy fires burn up your message. Get healing for your own wounds. We all have them, because we all live in a fallen world, and I can tell you that it has been liberating for me—after years of being way too defensive—to begin working from a healed and holy place. It has been much more effective and peace-bringing to stop trying to level the playing field and to simply be an orthodox-leaning woman who leads in ministry and who is not angry about it. Praise God for the healing he has brought! And please, God, heal me some more, because I'm not nearly who you've designed me to be. Not yet.

I think you already know all this, but maybe, on the tough days, it helps to hear it again.

That's the word I gave one day to a spiritual leader who was in need of empathy and encouragement. It's the word I will leave with all those who are contending bravely and faithfully for the gospel. If all we've discussed has been only for the purpose of proving our worth as women or making ourselves more comfortable in the roles we hold, I'm not sure this book would have been worth your time or mine. But it's about so much more. This work we're about is ultimately kingdom work. The reason we do what we do is not so people will learn to like women leaders, but so people will learn to worship Jesus Christ. This is the grand hope toward which we are all headed. It is that Jesus's own prayer might be realized in our day: "Your kingdom come, your will be done, on earth as it is in heaven" (Matt. 6:10). When we unleash the whole people of God to do the whole work of God throughout the whole world, the solemn hope is the realization of that prayer and the final, full expression of God's kingdom on earth.

In fact, the real question is not, "Should women lead or preach in churches?" This is a freedom question, but ultimately not a salvation question. The real question is, "How many people does God want to reach, and how many people is he willing to use to reach them?" What if all God's people who are equipped for the work are called to humbly proclaim Jesus to a lost and hurting world?

All his people—including you.

Do you remember my daughter's innocent question to me when she was just seven years old? "Mama, can boys be preachers, too?"[10] It is a beautiful question, reflecting the movement of God, who has given all kinds of people the call to preach, who has given every one of us a platform to suit our spiritual gifts. This is great news! Because Jesus sets people free, he is able to redeem us from the pits we've dug for ourselves so he can call us forth to spread the good news of freedom through Christ. As we come, he is able to present us before his glorious presence without fault. But it's even more than that! He is able to present us before his glorious presence with *great joy*!

He is the only God, our Savior. He is glorious. He is majestic. He is powerful. He has authority in this world and in the world to come. He is our Master and our Redeemer. He who is, who was, and who is to come is truth eternal.

Who wouldn't want to share that news? And who wouldn't want to hear it?

ACKNOWLEDGMENTS

I am most grateful to colleagues in ministry who have treated me with uncommon grace, respect, and care, who have included me in their discussions and group texts, checked on me often, prayed for me daily, and made this journey into leadership the joy that it is. That most of those colleagues are men only deepens my gratitude. While I can't name them all, I do want to acknowledge those who directly contributed to getting this book in print. Bryan Collier's insistence that I turn my doctoral study into a book is likely the only reason I persisted in seeking publication. I'm beyond grateful for his gift of "holy aggravation." Without J.D. Walt, I doubt I would ever have published anything. He was the first to open a door for me into the publishing world, and his prophetic encouragement and consistent advocacy of my gifts over two decades of ministry has made all the difference. J.D. and Andy Miller at Seedbed were my advocates at Zondervan, and I am more than grateful to them for opening that door and introducing me to Ryan Pazdur, a world-class editor.

Dr. Ben Witherington's brilliant dialogue over many years on this subject of women in ministry leadership is a gift to the church, and his oversight of my first exegetical work in this area helped release me into the joy of my calling. I was honored to have had Dr. Witherington, Dr. Sue Russell, and Dr. Scot McKnight read portions of an early draft, and to have had multiple conversations with Dr. Cheryl Bridges Johns on several subjects related to women in leadership. The collective wisdom of these scholars is immense. Kelly Capers, my sister-in-law, gave the generous gift of time and expertise, editing and asking great questions when this study was still in its early stages. Reverend Mandy Smith read, commented, and cared her way through many of these chapters, and helped me round off some sharp edges. Her stories, connections, and generally good spirit were (and are) invaluable. I am grateful to all those church planters, pastors, and business leaders who answered my surveys, took my phone calls, accepted my lunch requests, and helped make this material more than a hunch.

My dear, steadfast husband, Steve, read every word at least once, allowed countless hours of nonjudgmental space for the writing, and labored through the proper forms of notes and bibliographies (there is no love more sacrificial than the love that signs up for formatting notes and bibliographies). I'm grateful to my daughter, Claire, and her husband, Pierce Drake (my partner at *The Art of Holiness*), who shared in many conversations about women in ministry and helped me understand what it is like to have a mom who is also a pastor.

That I have anything at all to contribute to the conversation about what happens when women lead is a tribute to the beautiful people of Mosaic Church in Evans, Georgia, who have shaped me as a spiritual leader through their patience, faith, and love. Thank you for giving me space to write, and for teaching me how to love and be loved within the family of Jesus. Community *is* essential and without it, I would have nothing to say at all.

APPENDIX

For Further Reading

When you are ready to delve more deeply into the theological foundations of an egalitarian approach to women's spiritual leadership, here are a few good options to start with:

Cunningham, Loren, and David Joel Hamilton. *Why Not Women? A Fresh Look at Scripture on Women in Missions, Ministry, and Leadership.* Seattle, WA: YWAM Publishing, 2000.

Dale, Felicity, Peggy Batcheller-Hijar, Neil Cole, Jan Diss, Katie Driver, Dave Ferguson, Michael Frost, Alan Hirsch, Suzette Lambert, Floyd McClung, Julie Ross, Frank Viola, and Jon Zens. *The Black Swan Effect: A Response to Gender Hierarchy in the Church.* Carol Stream, IL: Tyndale House Publishers, 2007.

Grady, J. Lee. *Ten Lies the Church Tells Women: How the Bible Has Been Misused to Keep Women in Spiritual Bondage.* Lake Mary, FL: Charisma House, 2013.

James, Carolyn Custis. *Half the Church: Recapturing God's Global Vision for Women.* Grand Rapids: Zondervan, 2011.

Johnson, Alan, ed. *How I Changed My Mind about Women in Leadership: Compelling Stories from Prominent Evangelicals*. Grand Rapids: Zondervan, 2010.

Kolb, Deborah, Judith Williams, and Carol Frohlinger. *Her Place at the Table: A Woman's Guide to Negotiating Five Key Challenges to Leadership Success*. San Francisco: Jossey-Bass, 2010.

Leach, Tara Beth. *Emboldened: A Vision for Empowering Women in Ministry*. Downers Grove, IL: IVP, 2017.

Lederleitner, Mary. *Women in God's Mission: Accepting the Invitation to Serve and Lead*. Downers Grove, IL: IVP, 2018.

McKnight, Scot, and Laura Barringer. *A Church Called Tov: Forming a Goodness Culture That Resists Abuses of Power and Promotes Healing*. Carol Stream, IL: Tyndale House Publishers, 2020.

Payne, Philip B. *Man and Woman, One in Christ: An Exegetical and Theological Study of Paul's Letters*. Grand Rapids: Zondervan, 2015.

Pierce, Ronald, and Rebecca Groothuis, eds. *Discovering Biblical Equality: Complementarity Without Hierarchy*. Downers Grove, IL: IVP Academic, 2005.

Strickland, Danielle. *Better Together: How Women and Men Can Heal the Divide and Work Together to Transform the Future*. Nashville, TN: Thomas Nelson, 2020.

Witherington, Ben. *Women and the Genesis of Christianity*. New York: Cambridge University Press, 1990.

Witherington, Ben. *Women in the Ministry of Jesus: A Study of Jesus' Attitudes to Women and Their Roles as Reflected in His Earthly Life*. New York: Cambridge University Press, 1984.

NOTES

Introduction: A Sign from God

1. This story first appeared August 17, 2015, at my *Art of Holiness* blog: https://artofholiness.com/a-sign-from-god-2/.
2. Ed Stetzer and Warren Bird, "The State of Church Planting in the United States: Research Overview and Qualitative Study of Primary Church Planting Entities," *Journal of the American Society for Church Growth* 19, no. 2 (2008): 1–42, https://digitalarchives.apu.edu/jascg/vol19/iss2/2/.
3. "Do Economic or Industry Factors Affect Business Survival?," Small Business Administration, Office of Advocacy, June 2012, https://www.sba.gov/sites/default/files/Business-Survival.pdf.
4. Chad Otar. "What Percentage of Small Businesses Fail—And How Can You Avoid Being One of Them?" Forbes Online. Oct. 25, 2018, https://www.forbes.com/sites/forbesfinancecouncil/2018/10/25/what-percentage-of-small-businesses-fail-and-how-can-you-avoid-being-one-of-them/?sh=c5fdcfd43b5f.
5. Mere Sovick, "Strategies Female Small Business Owners Use to Succeed in Business," abstract (PhD diss., Walden University, 2017) https://scholarworks.waldenu.edu/dissertations/4331/.
6. Ibid.

7. "Gender Differences in Startup Financing," Small Business Administration, Office of Advocacy, accessed November 21, 2017, https://www.sba.gov/sites/default/files/files/Gender%20 Differences%20in%20Startup%20Financings.pdf.

8. "Survey of Business Owner Facts: Women-Owned Businesses in the United States," Small Business Administration, Office of Advocacy, accessed September 21, 2017, https://cdn .advocacy.sba.gov/wp-content/uploads/2019/06/10112558/ Women-Owned-Businesses-in-the-United-States.pdf.

9. Stetzer and Bird, "State of Church Planting," 2008.

10. Robin Ely, Herminia Ibarra, and Deborah Kolb, "Women Rising: The Unseen Barriers," *Harvard Business Review,* September 2013, https://hbr.org/2013/09/women-rising-the -unseen-barriers.

11. Ibid.

12. Bruce Metzger, *A Textual Commentary on the Greek New Testament* (Peabody, MA: Hendrickson Publishers, 2007), 65.

13. Ben Witherington, email to the author, February 26, 2018.

14. According to the Pew Research Center, "While many major religious denominations in the United States now allow women to pastor churches and synagogues, only 11% of American congregations were led by women in 2012, according to press reports of an upcoming National Congregations Study survey. That figure had not changed since 1998 [nor has it changed significantly from 2012 to the present]. Many of the nation's largest denominations, including Roman Catholics, Southern Baptists, Mormons (Latter-day Saints), and the Orthodox Church in America, do not ordain women or allow them to lead congregations." Among Protestants, Southern Baptists are the largest denomination in the US, with more than 14 million members. Worldwide, Catholics comprise slightly more than 50% of the total Christian population, while Orthodox Christians make up almost 12% of the total. Neither of

these traditions ordain women. These numbers alone should suffice to make the point that a great percentage of the Christian world continues to wrestle with the place of women in leadership roles. See David Masci, "The Divide Over Ordaining Women," Pew Research Center, September 9, 2014, https://www.pewresearch.org/fact-tank /2014/09/09/the-divide-over-ordaining-women/.

Part 1: Barriers to Women Leading

1. See the appendix for a bibliography of resources on a biblical defense of women's leadership.

Chapter 1: The Theological Barrier

1. *The Dictionary of Modern Proverbs*, comp. Charles Clay Doyle, Wolfgang Mieder, and Fred R. Shapiro (New Haven: Yale University Press, 2012), s.v. "Anecdote."
2. "Can Women Be Religious Leaders?", National Congregations Study, Association of Religion Data Archives website, accessed February 1, 2021, https://thearda.com/ConQS/qs _53.asp.
3. Michele Margolis and Michael Sances, "Who Really Gives? Partisanship and Charitable Giving in the United States," SSRN, August 9, 2013, https://ssrn.com/abstract =2148033.
4. John Piper and Wayne Grudem, *50 Crucial Questions: An Overview of Central Concerns about Manhood and Womanhood* (Wheaton, IL: Crossway, 2016), 10.
5. Kris Beckert, "Seeding a New Community of Women in Church Planting," Missio Alliance, August 13, 2015, https://www.missioalliance.org/seeding-a-new-community -of-women-in-church-planting/.
6. Pope John Paul II, *Man and Woman He Created Them: A Theology of the Body* (Boston: Pauline Books and Media, 2006) loc. 3417 and 3725 of 17,914, Kindle.

7. Bruce Ware, "Summaries of the Egalitarian and Complementarian Positions," The Council on Biblical Manhood and Womanhood, June 26, 2007, https://cbmw.org/2007/06/26/summaries-of-the-egalitarian-and-complementarian-positions/.

8. Neil Cole, "A Bold Hermeneutic," in Felicity Dale et al., *The Black Swan Effect: A Response to Gender Hierarchy in the Church* (Carol Stream, IL: Tyndale House Publishers, 2007), loc. 2743 of 4612, Kindle.

9. "Afghanistan-Literacy Rate, Adult Female," Trading Economics, accessed August 14, 2021, https://tradingeconomics.com/afghanistan/literacy-rate-adult-female-percent-of-females-ages-15-and-above-wb-data.html.

10. "Women and Girls' Education-Facts and Figures," UNESCO, March 8, 2014, http://www.unesco.org/new/en/unesco/events/prizes-and-celebrations/celebrations/international-days/international-womens-day-2014/women-ed-facts-and-figure/.

11. "The adult literacy rate for Pakistan is 65%, with males at 69% and females at 40%. Those for India are 63%, with males at 75% and females at 51%. Similarly, Bangladesh's adult literacy rate is 57%, with males at 61% and females at 52%. That of Nepal is 49%, with males at 73% and females at 48%. In Bhutan, it is 53%, with males at 65% and females at 99%." Abdul Rehman, Luan Jingdong, and Imran Hussain. "The Province-wise Literacy Rate in Pakistan and Its Impact on the Economy." *Pacific Science Review B: Humanities and Social Sciences.* Volume 1, Issue 3, November 2015, 140–144. As printed in *ScienceDirect.* https://www.sciencedirect.com/science/article/pii/S2405883116300247.

12. "Facts on Child Marriage," International Women's Health Coalition, accessed September 2, 2021, https://iwhc.org/resources/facts-child-marriage/.

13. "2019 U.S. National Human Trafficking Hotline Statistics," Polaris, accessed August 21, 2021, https://polarisproject.org /2019-us-national-human-trafficking-hotline-statistics/.

14. "Honour Killings: Statistics and Data," Honour Based Violence Awareness Network, accessed September 2, 2021, http://hbv-awareness.com/statistics-data/.

15. Maria Zafar, "16 Shocking Facts about Violence against Women and Girls," United Nations Office for the Coordination of Humanitarian Affairs, Dec. 7, 2020, https://reliefweb .int/report/world/16-shocking-facts-about-violence-against -women-and-girls.

16. Christopher P. Krebs, et al, "The Campus Sexual Assault (CSA) Study," National Institute of Justice, October 2007, https://www.ojp.gov/pdffiles1/nij/grants/221153.pdf.

17. Zafar.

18. "Against My Will: Defying the Practices that Harm Women and Girls and Undermine Equality," UNFPA, 2020, https://www.unfpa.org/sites/default/files/pub-pdf/UNFPA _PUB_2020_EN_State_of_World_Population.pdf, 50.

19. John Feng, "China Has Nearly 35 Million More Single Men Than Women," Newsweek, May 18, 2021, https://www .newsweek.com/china-has-nearly-35-million-more-single -men-women-1592486/.

20. Aarzoo Snigdha, "13 women die in India every day due to unsafe abortions," India Today, July 26, 2018, https://www .newsweek.com/china-has-nearly-35-million-more-single -men-women-1592486/.

21. "UN Women and the World Bank Unveil New Data Analysis on Women and Poverty," UN Women, November 9, 2017, https://www.unwomen.org/en/news/stories/2017/11/news-un -women-and-the-world-bank-unveil-new-data-analysis-on -women-and-poverty.

22. Jessica Semega, Melissa Kollar, John Creamer, and Abi- nash Mohanty. "Income and Poverty in the United States:

2018," United States Census Bureau, September 10, 2019, https://www.census.gov/library/publications/2019/demo/p60 -266.html.

23. Claire Cain Miller, "When Wives Earn More than Husbands, Neither Partner Likes to Admit It," *New York Times* online, July 17, 2018, https://www.nytimes.com/2018/07/17/upshot /when-wives-earn-more-than-husbands-neither-like-to-admit -it.html.

24. Marta Murray-Close and Misty L. Heggeness, "Manning Up and Womaning Down: How Husbands and Wives Report Their Earnings When She Earns More," Social, Economic, and Housing Statistics Division, United States Census Bureau, June 6, 2018, https://www.census.gov/content/dam/Census /library/working-papers/2018/demo/SEHSD-WP2018-20.pdf.

25. Manal Al-Sharif, "We Finally Won the Right to Drive in Saudi Arabia. But the Kingdom's War on Women Is Only Getting Worse," *Time*, April 10, 2019, https://time.com /5567330/saudi-arabia-women-rights-drive/.

26. Dale, *Black Swan Effect*, loc. 882 of 4612, Kindle.

27. John Piper, "Satan's Design in Reversing Male Leadership Role," *Desiring God*, December 19, 1983, https://www .desiringgod.org/articles/satans-design-in-reversing-male -leadership-role.

28. "The Double-Bind Dilemma for Women in Leadership: Damned If You Do, Doomed If You Don't," Catalyst, July 15, 2007, https://www.catalyst.org/research/the-double -bind-dilemma-for-women-in-leadership-damned-if-you-do -doomed-if-you-dont/.

29. Malcolm Gladwell, *Blink: The Power of Thinking without Thinking* (New York: Little, Brown, 2005), loc. 2116 of 3902, Kindle.

30. Gladwell, loc. 2130 of 3902, Kindle.

31. Gladwell, loc. 2131 of 3902, Kindle.

32. Gladwell, loc. 2139 and 2171 of 3902, Kindle.

33. Dale, *Black Swan Effect*, loc. 318 of 4612, Kindle.

Chapter 2: The Perception Barrier

1. Kathleen L. McGinn and Nicole Tempest, "Heidi Roizen," *Harvard Business School Case 800–228*, January 2000 (revised April 2010).
2. Shannon Kelley, "The Likability Problem," *Undecided* (blog), January 4, 2011, https:/undecidedthebook.wordpress .com/2011/01/04/the-likability-problem/.
3. Joanne Martin, "Gender-Related Material in the New Core Curriculum," Stanford Graduate School of Business, January 1, 2007, https://www.gsb.stanford.edu /experience/news-history/gender-related-material-new-core -curriculum.
4. Nitin Nohria and Rakesh Khurana, eds., *Handbook of Leadership Theory and Practice: An HBS Centennial Colloquium on Advancing Leadership* (Boston: Harvard University Business Press, 2010), 18.
5. Rebecca Riffkin, "Americans Still Prefer a Male Boss to a Female Boss," *Gallup* online, October 14, 2014, https://news.gallup.com/poll/178484/americans-prefer-male -boss-female-boss.aspx.
6. Ibid.
7. Malcolm Gladwell, *Blink: The Power of Thinking without Thinking* (New York: Little, Brown, 2005), loc. 996 of 3902, Kindle.
8. Ibid., loc. 2948 of 3902, Kindle.
9. Ibid.
10. Ibid., loc. 2969 of 3902, Kindle.
11. Ibid., loc. 947 of 3902, Kindle.
12. Robin Ely, Herminia Ibarra, and Deborah Kolb, "Women Rising: The Unseen Barriers," *Harvard Business Review*, September 2013, https://hbr.org/2013/09/women-rising-the -unseen-barriers.

13. Herminia Ibarra and Jennifer Petriglieri, "Impossible Selves: Image Strategies and Identity Threat in Professional Women's Career Transitions" (working paper, INSEAD, March 2016), http://dx.doi.org/10.2139/ssrn.2742061.

14. "The Double-Bind Dilemma for Women in Leadership: Damned If You Do, Doomed If You Don't," Catalyst, July 15, 2007, https://www.catalyst.org/research/infographic-the -double-bind-dilemma-for-women-in-leadership/.

15. Robin Ely and Deborah L. Rhode, "Women and Leadership: Defining the Challenges," in *Handbook of Leadership Theory and Practice*, eds. Nitin Nohria and Rakesh Khurana (Boston: Harvard Business Press, 2010), 385.

16. "The Double-Bind Dilemma for Women in Leadership," 13.

17. Soares and Mulligan-Ferry, "2013 Catalyst Census: Fortune 500 Women Executive Officers and Top Earners," Catalyst, https://www.catalyst.org/wp-content/uploads /2019/02/2013_catalyst_census_fortune_500_women _executive_officers_top_earners.pdf.

18. Deborah Rhode, *Women and Leadership* (London: Oxford University Press, 2017), 63.

19. Robert Safian, "'I Knew I Would Get Fired': Sallie Krawcheck," Fast Company, October 14, 2014, https://www .fastcompany.com/3036587/i-knew-i-would-get-fired-sallie -krawcheck.

20. "Sallie Krawcheck," Ellevate Network, accessed February 2, 2021, https://www.ellevatenetwork.com/team/sallie -krawcheck.

21. Because it is a human tendency to gravitate toward others with whom one has common interests and affinities, strong male leaders are more likely to be attracted to other strong male leaders, leaving women with the challenge of attracting effective leadership teams. In other words, men prefer to relate to other men while failing to take note of the

contributions of women. See Ely, Ibarra, and Kolb, "Women Rising: The Unseen Barriers."

22. Rhode, "Women and Leadership," 397.

23. Sheryl Sandberg, "Why We Have Too Few Women Leaders," TED video, 14:42, December 2010, https://www.ted.com/talks/sheryl_sandberg_why_we_have_too_few_women_leaders.

24. Ibid.

25. Glynis M. Breakwell, "Resisting Representations and Identity Processes," *Papers on Social Representations* 19 (2010): 6.1-6.11, https://purehost.bath.ac.uk/ws/portalfiles/portal/310607/PSR_19_06Breakwell.pdf.

26. Blake E. Ashforth and Glen E. Kreiner, "'How Can You Do It?': Dirty Work and the Challenge of Constructing a Positive Identity," *Academy of Management Review* 24, no. 3 (July 1999), https://doi.org/10.5465/amr.1999.2202129.

27. Carol Gilligan, *In a Different Voice: Psychological Theory and Women's Development* (Cambridge: Harvard University Press, 1982), 160.

28. R. M. Arkin, "Self-Presentation Styles," in *Impression Management Theory and Social Psychological Research*, ed. J. T. Tedeschi (New York: Academic Press, 1981), 311–333.

29. Ashforth and Kreiner, "Constructing a Positive Identity," 413.

30. Carolyn Moore, "At the Intersection of Acts and Galatians: New Strategies for Women Church Planters" (DMin dissertation, Asbury Theological Seminary, 2018), 57.

31. Ely, Ibarra, and Kolb, "Women Rising."

32. Brian Ross, ed., *The Psychology of Learning and Motivation, Volume 61* (Salt Lake City: Academic Press, 2014), 75.

33. Tali Sharot, *The Optimism Bias: Why We're Wired to Look on the Bright Side* (London: Constable & Robinson, 2012).

34. Tali Sharot, "The Optimism Bias," TED video, 17:24,

February 2012, https://www.ted.com/talks/tali_sharot_the
_optimism_bias.

35. James A. Shepperd et al., "Taking Stock of Unrealistic
Optimism," *Perspectives on Psychological Science* 8, no. 4
(July 2013): 395–411.

36. Ibid.

37. Moore, "New Strategies for Women Church Planters," 166.

38. Felicity Dale et al., *The Black Swan Effect: A Response to
Gender Hierarchy in the Church* (Carol Stream, IL: Tyndale
House Publishers, 2007), loc. 882 of 4612, Kindle.

Chapter 3: Resources and Benchmarks

1. "What Americans Think about Women in Power," Barna
Group: Research Releases in Leaders & Pastors, March 8,
2017, https://www.barna.com/research/americans-think
-women-power/.

2. Ibid. According to the Barna report, there are no reliable
statistics on the percentage of women among church
planters. (A written query of the Barna Group received
this response: "Sorry, no data in our recent study. But on
average, 10% of Protestant churches are led by females.") A
very unofficial estimate offered by Dr. Ed Stetzer—formerly
of LifeWay Research and currently the Billy Graham Chair
of Church, Mission, and Evangelism at Wheaton College
and Executive Director of the Billy Graham Center—is less
than 5 percent.

3. Alyssa Newcomb, "Record Number of Women Took
Over Fortune 500 Companies in 2020," NBC News,
December 30, 2020, https://www.nbcnews.com/business
/business-news/record-number-women-took-over-fortune
-500-companies-2020-n1252491. This article notes a
phenomenon that holds true for women recruited to lead
many larger companies: "A record number of women took
over as CEO in 2020 to help steer their company through

an uncertain and volatile business environment prompted by the coronavirus pandemic. Women are more likely to be elevated to positions of leadership in times of crisis and downturn, but are essentially taking on a higher risk for failure, according to a phenomenon known as the 'glass cliff.'" See also this article in the *Wall Street Journal* for a different (and lower) statistic on the number of women leading Fortune 500 companies: Dana Mattioli and Cara Lombardo, "Walgreens Poaches Starbucks Executive Rosalind Brewer for CEO," January 26, 2021, https://www.wsj.com/articles/walgreens-to-name-starbucks-executive-roz-brewer-as-ceo-11611700794.

4. Robin Ely, Herminia Ibarra, and Deborah Kolb, "Women Rising: The Unseen Barriers," *Harvard Business Review*, September 2013, https://hbr.org/2013/09/women-rising-the-unseen-barriers.

5. Belle Rose Ragins and John L. Cotton, "Easier Said than Done: Gender Differences in Perceived Barriers to Gaining a Mentor," *The Academy of Management Journal 1991*, 34, no. 4 (December 1991): 939–51, https://doi.org/10.2307/256398.

6. Richard C. Nemanick, Jr., "Comparing Formal and Informal Mentors: Does Type Make a Difference?," *The Academy of Management Executive* 14, no. 3 (August 2000): 136–38, https://www.jstor.org/stable/4165667.

7. Nicole Williams, "Women and Mentoring: LinkedIn Study," Pennsylvania Conference for Women, accessed February 2, 2021, https://www.paconferenceforwomen.org/women-and-mentoring-linkedin-study/.

8. Michel Martin, "Why Do So Few Women Have Mentors?: Interview with Nicole Williams," NPR, December 14, 2011, https://www.npr.org/2011/12/14/143707496/why-do-so-few-women-have-mentors.

9. Ibid.

10. "What Americans Think About Women in Power," Barna Group.

11. Quotes by women pastors and denominational leaders in this chapter are all taken from the written survey and interviews I conducted in 2017–2018 for my dissertation at Asbury Theological Seminary: "At the Intersection of Acts and Galatians: New Strategies for Women Church Planters," 2018.

12. Herminia Ibarra, "A Lack of Sponsorship Is Keeping Women from Advancing into Leadership," *Harvard Business Review*, August 19, 2019, https://hbr.org/2019/08 /a-lack-of-sponsorship-is-keeping-women-from-advancing -into-leadership.

13. Susan Vinnicombe and Val Singh, "Women-only Management Training: An Essential Part of Women's Leadership Development," *Journal of Change Management* 3, no. 4 (2002): 294–306, https://doi.org/10.1080/714023846.

14. "What Americans Think About Women in Power," Barna Group.

15. Robin Ely and Deborah L. Rhode, "Women and Leadership: Defining the Challenges," in *Handbook of Leadership Theory and Practice*, eds. Nitin Nohria and Rakesh Khurana (Boston: Harvard Business Press, 2010), 377–410.

16. Ibid., 380.

17. Ely, Ibarra, and Kolb, "Women Rising."

18. Kim Parker et al., "Women and Leadership: Public Says Women are Equally Qualified, but Barriers Persist," Pew Research Center, January 2015, https://assets.pewresearch .org/wp-content/uploads/sites/3/2015/01/2015-01-14 _women-and-leadership.pdf, 31.

19. Ibid., 34.

20. Ibid., 34–35.

21. Ex. 1:11–14, 5:6–18.

22. Luke 9:3–5.

23. Ps. 50:10.

Chapter 4: The Pastoral Care Barrier

1. Bob Smietana, "For Some Pastors, the Past Year Was a Sign from God It Was Time to Quit," Religion News Service, May 7, 2021, https://religionnews.com/2021/05/07/for-some -pastors-the-past-year-was-a-sign-that-it-was-time-to-quit/.
2. Carey Nieuwhof, "How Pastoral Care Stunts the Growth of Most Churches," *Carey Nieuwhof* (blog), November 16, 2015, https://careynieuwhof.com/how-pastoral-care-stunts -the-growth-of-most-churches/.
3. Carol Gilligan, *In a Different Voice: Psychological Theory and Women's Development* (Cambridge: Harvard University Press, 1982), loc. 122 of 4002, Kindle.
4. Ibid., loc. 335 of 4002, Kindle.
5. Ibid., loc. 598 of 4002, Kindle.
6. Mary Field Belenky et al., *Women's Ways of Knowing: The Development of Self, Voice, and Mind* (New York: Basic Books, 2008), loc. 808 of 3614, Kindle.
7. Emma Ineson, "Transforming Power: Is there a 'Feminine' Style of Leadership?" *Anvil* 17, no. 2 (2000): 124, https://biblicalstudies.org.uk/pdf/anvil/17-2_121.pdf.
8. Ibid.
9. Carey Nieuwhof, "5 Pastoral Emergencies That Aren't Emergencies," *Carey Nieuwhof* (blog), accessed May 5, 2022, https://careynieuwhof.com/5-pastoral-emergencies -that-arent-emergencies/.
10. Simon Sinek, *Leaders Eat Last: Why Some Teams Pull Together and Others Don't* (New York: Portfolio Penguin, 2017), loc. 918 of 4690, Kindle.
11. Nieuwhof, "How Pastoral Care Stunts Growth."
12. Carolyn Moore, "At the Intersection of Acts and Galatians: New Strategies for Women Church Planters" (DMin dissertation, Asbury Theological Seminary, 2018), 125.
13. Edward Morgan, III, "Implications of the Masculine and the Feminine in Pastoral Ministry," *Journal of Pastoral Care*

34, no. 4 (December 1980): 273, https://doi.org/10.1177%2
F002234098003400407.

14. Josh Huynh, "Bob Newhart - Stop It," YouTube video, 6:20,
https://www.youtube.com/watch?v=Ow0lr63y4Mw.

15. Of course, my nurturing side won't let me leave this
comment there without mentioning that in survey after
survey, my folks note the warmhearted personality of our
community. We are a "come as you are" kind of church.
We've just learned how to spread pastoral care around so it
doesn't all fall on the pastor.

16. "Co-Dependency," Mental Health America, accessed July 1,
2021, https://www.mhanational.org/co-dependency.

17. Some of my favorites, if you're ready to go deeper, are:
*Codependent No More: How to Stop Controlling Others
and Start Caring for Yourself* by Melody Beattie (I don't
think you can go wrong with anything she has published,
and she has published a lot); *The Road Back to Me:
Healing and Recovering From Co-dependency, Addiction,
Enabling, and Low Self Esteem* by Lisa A. Romano; and
*Please Don't Say You Need Me: Biblical Answers for
Codependency* by Jan Silvious.

18. Morgan, "Masculine and Feminine," 273.

19. Moore, "New Strategies for Women Church Planters," 105.

20. Erich Neumann, *The Great Mother: An Analysis of the
Archetype* (New York: Princeton University Press, 1983).

21. Moore, "New Strategies for Women Church Planters," 125.

22. Devrupa Rakshit, "Why People with a Savior Complex
Sacrifice Their Own Needs to Help Others," The Swaddle
(website), December 25, 2020, https://theswaddle.com/why
-people-with-a-savior-complex-sacrifice-their-own-needs-to
-help-others/.

23. Harriet B. Braiker, *The Type E Woman: How to Overcome
the Stress of Being Everything to Everybody* (London:
Penguin Publishing Group, 1987).

24. Susan Vinnicombe and Val Singh, "Women-only Management Training: An Essential Part of Women's Leadership Development," *Journal of Change Management* 3, no. 4 (2002): 303, https://doi.org/10.1080/714023846.

25. Dorothy Littell Greco, "My Biggest Ministry Mistake," WomenLeaders.com, *Christianity Today*, February 14, 2017, https://www.christianitytoday.com/women-leaders /2017/february/my-biggest-ministry-mistake.html?start=1.

26. Katherine Willis Pershey, "When Men Misinterpret Pastoral Care," WomenLeaders.com, *Christianity Today*, November 11, 2013, https://www.christianitytoday.com /women-leaders/2013/november/when-men-misinterpret -pastoral-care.html?start=1.

Chapter 5: The Biological Barrier

1. The median age for a first marriage is twenty-eight for women and thirty for men. In 1960, the median age of marriage for women was twenty. Historically, this is a huge jump and represents a trend toward reversing family and career. Women are deferring marriage while they develop their careers at a much greater rate than previous generations. See "Median Age at First Marriage: 1890 to Present," U. S. Census Bureau, accessed February 8, 2021, https://www .census.gov/content/dam/Census/library/visualizations/time -series/demo/families-and-households/ms-2.pdf.

2. Lisa Selin Davis, "In Her Words: 'Women Do It All,'" In Her Words, *New York Times*, May 30, 2021, https://my newsresources.blogspot.com/2021/05/in-her-words-women -do-it-all.html.

3. Cheryl Bridges Johns, telephone interview with the author, May 21, 2021.

4. Carolyn Moore, "At the Intersection of Acts and Galatians: New Strategies for Women Church Planters" (DMin dissertation, Asbury Theological Seminary, 2018), 118–119.

5. Ibid.

6. Ibid.

7. Robin Ely and Irene Padavic, "What's Really Holding Women Back?," *Harvard Business Review*, March–April 2020, https://hbr.org/2020/03/whats-really-holding-women -back.

8. F. M. Cheung and D. F. Halpern, "Women at the Top: Powerful Leaders Define Success as Work + Family in a Culture of Gender," *American Psychologist* 65, no. 43 (2010): 182, https://doi.org/10.1037/a0017309.

9. Sheryl Sandberg, "Why We Have Too Few Women Leaders," TED video, 14:42, December 2010, https://www .ted.com/talks/sheryl_sandberg_why_we_have_too_few _women_leaders.

10. Ely and Padavic, "What's Really Holding Women Back?"

11. Amanda Sinclair, *Doing Leadership Differently: Gender, Power and Sexuality in a Changing Business Culture* (Carlton Victoria, Australia: Melbourne University Press, 2004), 103.

12. Johns, telephone interview, May 21, 2021.

13. Moore, "New Strategies for Women Church Planters," 117–118.

14. Ely and Padavic, "What's Really Holding Women Back?"

15. Juliana Menasce Horowitz, Nikki Graf, and Gretchen Livingston, "The Landscape of Marriage and Cohabitation in the U.S.," Pew Research Center, November 6, 2019, https://www.pewresearch.org/social-trends/2019/11/06/the -landscape-of-marriage-and-cohabitation-in-the-u-s/.

16. Kendra Cherry, "Intimacy vs. Isolation: Psychosocial Stage 6," Verywell Mind, updated November 4, 2020, https://www .verywellmind.com/intimacy-versus-isolation-2795739. In addition to this source, there are multiple articles and books online on Erik Erikson's Theory of Psychosocial Development and Stage 6: Intimacy vs. Isolation.

17. Moore, "New Strategies for Women Church Planters," 123.
18. Ely and Padavic, "What's Really Holding Women Back?"
19. Sinclair, *Doing Leadership Differently*, 77.
20. Johns, telephone interview, May 21, 2021.
21. Mandy Smith and Zoe Smith, "Imagining the Next Generation of Women in Leadership: A Conversation between a Lead Pastor and Her Daughter," WomenLeaders .com, *Christianity Today*, August 10, 2017, https://www .christianitytoday.com/women-leaders/2017/august /imagining-next-generation-of-women-in-leadership.html.
22. Moore, "New Strategies for Women Church Planters," 120.
23. Colette Bouchez, "Your Brain on Menopause," WebMD, updated August 2006, https://www.webmd.com/menopause /features/your-brain-on-menopause.
24. Cheryl Bridges Johns, *Seven Transforming Gifts of Menopause: An Unexpected Spiritual Journey* (Ada, MI: Brazos Press, 2020), 30.
25. Ibid., 40.
26. Ibid., 42.
27. Moore, "New Strategies for Women Church Planters," 122–123.
28. Email message to the author, January 3, 2017.
29. Sinclair, *Doing Leadership Differently*, xi.

Part 2: Empowering Women to Lead and Succeed

1. Jim Collins, *Good to Great* (New York: HarperCollins Business, 2001), 210.

Chapter 6: Identity

1. Carolyn Moore, "At the Intersection of Acts and Galatians: New Strategies for Women Church Planters" (DMin dissertation, Asbury Theological Seminary, 2018), 129.
2. Ibid.

3. Ibid., 130.

4. Hee An Choi and Jacqueline Blue, "United Methodist Clergywomen Retention Study II in the U.S. Context," Anna Howard Shaw Center, Boston University, accessed June 15, 2021, https://www.bu.edu/shaw/publications/united -methodist-clergywomen-retention-study-ii-2/.

5. I am grateful to Rick Sholette, a therapist in Evans, Georgia, for introducing me to this exercise.

6. Neil Anderson, *Who I Am in Christ*, rev. ed. (Minneapolis: Bethany House Publishers, 2001), 10–11.

7. Robin Ely, Herminia Ibarra, and Deborah Kolb, "Women Rising: The Unseen Barriers," *Harvard Business Review*, September 2013, https://hbr.org/2013/09/women-rising-the -unseen-barriers.

8. Ian Morgan Cron and Suzanne Stabile, *The Road Back to You: An Enneagram Journey to Self-Discovery* (Downers Grove, IL: IVP Books, 2016).

9. Ibid., 11, 15.

10. Reginald Johnson, *Your Personality and the Spiritual Life* (Gainesville, FL: Center for Applications of Psychological Type, 1999), loc. 113 of 2736, Kindle.

11. Edgar H. Schein, *Career Anchors: Discovering Your Real Values* (San Diego: Pfeiffer, 1990), 1.

12. Ibid., 26.

13. Johnson, *Personality and Spiritual Life*, loc. 232 of 2736, Kindle.

Chapter 7: Authority

1. "Learned Behaviors: Monologue," *The Small Bow* 3, no. 28 (2021), https://www.thesmallbow.com/campaigns/view -campaign/q7ghSxhFeYIlJ3DDdqtj2QnOOzW_pohbmFTp Z6G7R-KiRakgzhM1uhFWyZrLRCQ-q_KkJsb4CebpICZ V5-ymNbuxKJWGvYAU.

2. Susan Vinnicombe and Val Singh, "Women-only

Management Training: An Essential Part of Women's Leadership Development," *Journal of Change Management* 3, no. 4 (2002): 304, https://doi.org/10.1080/714023846.

3. A. H. Eagly, M. C. Johannesen-Schmidt, and M. L. van Engen, "Transformational, Transactional, and Laissez-Faire Leadership Styles: A Meta-Analysis Comparing Women and Men," *Psychological Bulletin* 129, no. 4 (2003): 569–591, https://doi.org/10.1037/0033-2909.129.4.569.

4. Claire Cain Miller, "When Wives Earn More Than Husbands, Neither Partner Likes to Admit It," *New York Times* online, July 17, 2018, https://www.nytimes.com/2018/07/17/upshot/when-wives-earn-more-than-husbands-neither-like-to-admit-it.html.

5. Eagly, Johannesen-Schmidt, and van Engen, "Transformational, Transactional, and Laissez-Faire Leadership Styles," 570.

6. Madeline E. Heilman and Tyler G. Okimoto, "Why Are Women Penalized for Success at Male Tasks?: The Implied Communality Deficit," *Journal of Applied Psychology* 92, no. 1 (January 1, 2007): 81–92, https://psycnet.apa.org/doi/10.1037/0021-9010.92.1.81.

7. Eagly, Johannesen-Schmidt, and van Engen, "Transformational, Transactional, and Laissez-Faire Leadership Styles," 586.

8. Ibid., 589.

9. Vinnicombe and Singh, "Women-only Management Training," 302.

10. Ibid., 298.

11. Ruth Sealy and Val Singh, "Healthy Mentoring: The Importance of Role Models in the Development of Leaders' Professional Identities," in *Leadership Perspectives: Knowledge into Action*, eds. Kim Turnbull James and James Collins (New York: Macmillan, 2008), 208.

12. *Toy Story*, directed by John Lasseter, voice performances

by Tom Hanks and Tim Allen (Burbank, CA: Walt Disney Pictures and Pixar Animation Studios, 1995).

13. Steve Kempster, Marian Iszatt-White, and Matt Brown, "Authenticity in Leadership: Reframing Relational Transparency through the Lens of Emotional Labour," *Leadership* 15, no. 3 (2019): 319, https://doi.org/10.1177 %2F1742715017746788.

14. Ibid., 320.

15. Ibid., 321.

16. Email message to the author, September 30, 2013.

17. Larry Crabb, *Connecting: Healing Ourselves and Our Relationships* (Nashville: Thomas Nelson, 1997), 65.

Chapter 8: Equipping

1. Ed Stetzer and Warren Bird, "The State of Church Planting in the United States: Research Overview and Qualitative Study of Primary Church Planting Entities," *Journal of the American Society for Church Growth* 19, no. 2 (2008): 1–42, https://digitalarchives.apu.edu/jascg/vol19/iss2/2/.

2. "Do Economic or Industry Factors Affect Business Survival?," Small Business Administration, Office of Advocacy, June 2012, https://www.sba.gov/sites/default/files /Business-Survival.pdf.

3. Mere Sovick, "Strategies Female Small Business Owners Use to Succeed in Business" abstract (PhD diss., Walden University, 2017) https://scholarworks.waldenu.edu /dissertations/4331/.

4. Stetzer and Bird, "State of Church Planting."

5. Jeff Atwood, "The Danger of Naïveté," *Coding Horror* (blog), December 7, 2007, https://blog.codinghorror.com/the -danger-of-naivete/.

6. See my complete blog article on this topic: Carolyn Moore, "Developing Givers in the Kingdom of God," *Art of*

Holiness (blog), November 16, 2016, https://artofholiness
.com/developing-givers-in-the-kingdom-of-god/.

7. Barbara Stanny, *Secrets of Six-Figure Women: Surprising Strategies to Up Your Earnings and Change Your Life* (New York: HarperCollins, 2004), 59.

8. "Are Salary Negotiation Skills Different for Men and Women?," Harvard Law School: Program on Negotiation Daily Blog, July 8, 2021, https://www.pon.harvard.edu/daily /salary-negotiations/salary-negotiation-skills-different-for -men-and-women/.

9. Kristen Senz, "Salary Negotiations: A Catch-22 for Women," Harvard Business School: Working Knowledge, April 2, 2021, https://hbswk.hbs.edu/item/salary-negotiations-a-catch -22-for-women.

10. Leslie Knight, *Career Strategies for Christian Women: Negotiate the Salary You Deserve* self-pub., (CreateSpace Publishing, 2015), 20.

11. Moore, "Developing Givers in the Kingdom."

12. Carolyn Moore, "At the Intersection of Acts and Galatians: New Strategies for Women Church Planters" (DMin dissertation, Asbury Theological Seminary, 2018), 112.

13. Trisha Taylor, email message to Mandy Smith, forwarded to the author on May 23, 2021.

14. Susan Vinnicombe and Val Singh, "Women-only Management Training: An Essential Part of Women's Leadership Development," *Journal of Change Management* 3, no. 4 (2002): 300, https://doi.org/10.1080/714023846.

15. Ibid.

16. This phrase comes from the movie *Chariots of Fire*, directed by Hugh Hudson, starring Ben Cross and Ian Charleson, (Los Angeles: 20th Century Fox, 1981). The scene in which Eric Liddell tells his sister, "When I run, I feel [God's] pleasure," is worth watching: Mike McPharlin, "God Made

Me Fast," YouTube video, 1:02, April 19, 2016, https://www
.youtube.com/watch?v=ile5PD34SS0.

Chapter 9: Partnership

1. Susan Vinnicombe and Val Singh, "Women-only
   Management Training: An Essential Part of Women's
   Leadership Development," *Journal of Change Management*
   3, no. 4 (2002): 304, https://doi.org/10.1080/714023846.
2. Ibid.
3. John Whitmore, *Coaching for Performance: Growing
   People, Performance and Purpose* (London: Nicholas
   Brealey Publishing, 2002), 8.
4. Tony Stoltzfus, *Leadership Coaching: The Disciplines,
   Skills and Heart of a Christian Coach*, self-pub.
   (CreateSpace Publishing, 2005), 6.
5. Whitmore, *Coaching for Performance*, 12.
6. Ibid., 12.
7. Jorge Acevedo, email message to the author, July 11, 2021.
8. Carolyn Moore, "At the Intersection of Acts and Galatians:
   New Strategies for Women Church Planters" (DMin
   dissertation, Asbury Theological Seminary, 2018), 134.
9. Ibid.
10. Nicole Williams, "Women and Mentoring: LinkedIn
    Study," Pennsylvania Conference for Women, accessed
    February 2, 2021, https://www.paconferenceforwomen.org
    /women-and-mentoring-linkedin-study/.
11. Vinnicombe and Singh, "Women-only Management
    Training," 297–298.
12. Ibid., 297.
13. Antoinette G. Alvarado, *My Sister's Keeper: A Strategic
    Leadership Coaching Model for the Identity Formation
    of Women in Leadership at Total Grace Christian Center*
    (Charleston, SC: Proquest, 2011).
14. "The Double-Bind Dilemma for Women in Leadership:

Damned If You Do, Doomed If You Don't," Catalyst, July 15, 2007, https://www.catalyst.org/research/the-double -bind-dilemma-for-women-in-leadership-damned-if-you-do -doomed-if-you-dont/. See also, Herminia Ibarra and Jennifer Petriglieri, "Impossible Selves: Image Strategies and Identity Threat in Professional Women's Career Transitions" (working paper, INSEAD, March 2016), http://dx.doi.org /10.2139/ssrn.2742061; and Simon Sinek, *Leaders Eat Last: Why Some Teams Pull Together and Others Don't* (New York: Portfolio, 2014), 171.

15. Robin Ely and Deborah L. Rhode, "Women and Leadership: Defining the Challenges," in *Handbook of Leadership Theory and Practice*, eds. Nitin Nohria and Rakesh Khurana (Boston: Harvard Business Press, 2010), 381. See also, "The Double-Bind Dilemma," Catalyst, July 15, 2007.

16. Vinnicombe and Singh, "Women-only Management Training," 302.

17. Ibid., 297.

18. Ruth Sealy and Val Singh, "Healthy Mentoring: The Importance of Role Models in the Development of Leaders' Professional Identities," in *Leadership Perspectives: Knowledge in Action*, eds. Kim Turnbull James and James Collins (New York: Macmillan, 2008), 208–222.

19. Vinnicombe and Singh, "Women-only Management Training," 297.

20. Moore, "New Strategies for Women Church Planters," 134.

21. Vinnicombe and Singh, "Women-only Management Training," 302.

22. Herminia Ibarra, "A Lack of Sponsorship Is Keeping Women from Advancing into Leadership," *Harvard Business Review*, August 19, 2019, https://hbr.org/2019/08 /a-lack-of-sponsorship-is-keeping-women-from-advancing -into-leadership.

23. Moore, "New Strategies for Women Church Planters," 137.

24. Portions of this section were excerpted from Carolyn Moore, "Holiness and the Billy Graham Rule," *Art of Holiness* (blog), March 31, 2017, https://artofholiness.com /holiness-and-the-billy-graham-rule/.

25. Laura Turner, "The Religious Reasons Mike Pence Won't Eat Alone with Women Don't Add Up," *Washington Post*, March 30, 2017, https://www.washingtonpost.com/news /acts-of-faith/wp/2017/03/30/the-religious-reasons-mike -pence-wont-eat-alone-with-women-dont-add-up/.

26. Bryan Collier, email message to the author, July 11, 2021.

Chapter 10: It's All about the Kingdom of God

1. Jim Collins, *Good to Great: Why Some Companies Make the Leap and Others Don't* (New York: HarperCollins Business, 2001), 210.

2. Carolyn Moore, "At the Intersection of Acts and Galatians: New Strategies for Women Church Planters" (DMin dissertation, Asbury Theological Seminary, 2018), 152.

3. A version of this story (written by the author) first appeared as "Men, Women, and the Kingdom of God," *Good News Magazine*, November 26, 2018, https://goodnewsmag.org /2018/11/men-women-and-the-kingdom-of-god/.

4. Sinead O'Carroll, "'Unwanted' Indian Girls Change Their Names in Special Ceremony," *The Journal*, October 23, 2011, https://www.thejournal.ie/unwanted-indian-girls -change-their-names-in-special-ceremony-261130-Oct2011/.

5. "Women as Preachers: Evangelical Precedents," *Christianity Today*, May 23, 1975, https://www.christianitytoday.com /ct/1975/may-23/women-as-preachers-evangelical-precedents .html.

6. Timothy Tennent, "Lecture 3 in Essentials of World Missions: Theological Questions," Biblical Training, accessed September 12, 2020, https://www.biblicaltraining .org/transcriptions/lecture-3-theological-questions.

7. This teaching on Paul and Acts 16 was first delivered to the Wesleyan Covenant Association Global Gathering on May 1, 2021. The text of that talk was subsequently published by *Good News Magazine*. See Carolyn Moore, "Hope on the Horizon," *Good News Magazine*, July 26, 2021, https://goodnewsmag.org/2021/07/hope-on-the-horizon/.

8. This phenomenon is detailed in the movie *Sheep Among Wolves Volume II*, directed by Dalton Thomas (Jackson, WY: FAI Studios, 2019). See also the article about the movie: Caleb Parke, "Iran Has World's 'Fastest-Growing Church,' Despite No Buildings—and It's Mostly Led by Women: Documentary," Fox News, September 27, 2019, https://www.foxnews.com/faith-values/worlds-fastest-growing-church-women-documentary-film.

9. Felicity Dale et al., *The Black Swan Effect: A Response to Gender Hierarchy in the Church* (Carol Stream, IL: Tyndale House Publishers, 2007), loc. 318 of 4612, Kindle.

10. This memory was first shared in a blog post. See Carolyn Moore, "'Mama, Can Boys Be Preachers, Too?,'" *Art of Holiness*, June 27, 2016, http://artofholiness.com/until-all-hear/.